THE ENIGMA OF THE
freemasons

THEIR HISTORY AND MYSTICAL CONNECTIONS

THE ENIGMA OF THE
freemasons

THEIR HISTORY AND MYSTICAL CONNECTIONS

TIM WALLACE-MURPHY

Published by The Disinformation Company Ltd.
163 Third Avenue, Suite 108
New York, NY 10003
Tel.: +1.212.691.1605
Fax: +1.212.691.1606
www.disinfo.com

Library of Congress Control Number: 2006925222

ISBN-10: 1-932857-44-3
ISBN-13: 978-1-932857-44-3

Printed in China

10 9 8 7 6 5 4 3 2 1

This book was conceived, designed, and produced by
IXOS PRESS LIMITED an imprint of IVY PRESS LIMITED
The Old Candlemakers, West Street,
Lewes, East Sussex BN7 2NZ, U.K.
www.ivy-group.co.uk

Publisher: David Alexander
Creative Director: Peter Bridgewater
Art Director: Kevin Knight
Editorial Director: Caroline Earle
Senior Project Editor: Rebecca Saraceno
Designer: Nicola Liddiard
Project Designer: Joanna Clinch
Picture Researcher: Shelley Noronha

Distributed in the USA and Canada by:
Consortium Book Sales and Distribution
1045 Westgate Drive, Suite 90
St Paul, MN 55114
Toll Free: +1.800.283.3572 Local: +1.651.221.9035 Fax: +1.651.221.0124
www.cbsd.com

contents

INTRODUCTION   6

THE CRADLE OF CULTURE   8

THE BIRTH OF CHRISTIANITY   16

HIDDEN STREAMS OF SPIRITUALITY   22

THE MEDIEVAL CRAFTMASONS   32

THE HOLY GRAIL AND THE TEMPLARS   40

SCOTTISH BEGINNINGS   50

EMBRYONIC FREEMASONRY   60

CONSOLIDATION AND DIVISION   68

THE HUMAN CATALYST   76

FREEMASONS' INFLUENCE ON SOCIETY   84

EIGHTEENTH-CENTURY DEVELOPMENTS IN EUROPE   96

GLIMPSES FROM WITHIN   106

BROTHERHOOD AND CHARITY   116

A DEGREE OF TRUTH?   122

FURTHER READING   130

GLOSSARY   132

INDEX   138

ACKNOWLEDGMENTS   144

introduction

THE FREEMASONS ARE A SECRETIVE, WORLD-WIDE BROTHERHOOD, SHROUDED IN MYSTERY AND CLOTHED IN CONTROVERSY. THE TRUTH ABOUT THIS FRATERNITY IS FAR MORE FASCINATING THAN ANY FICTION.

M ention the word "Freemasonry" in any conversation and stand by for a strongly opinionated response. This is far from surprising, for Freemasonry has often been viewed with suspicion by the Church/State establishment throughout Europe, is frequently targeted by the tabloid press with accusations of corruption, has been linked with worldwide Jewry as the source of all the world's evils by conspiracy theorists, and has been subject to condemnation by the Catholic Church for centuries. Indeed, the Church, at one time, imposed the death penalty for any citizen of the Papal States who became a member. Yet, many historians credit individual Freemasons with creating that beacon of democracy, the Constitution of the United States; they also state categorically that Freemasons played a major role in the campaign that led to the unification of Italy; were prominent among the courageous liberators of many states in South America; and made a massive contribution to European culture with the works of Goethe, Mozart, and, some would even claim, Beethoven.

According to the United Grand Lodge of England, Freemasonry sprang fully formed out of some mythical vacuum in the late seventeenth and early eighteenth centuries with its basic rituals and teaching intact—a story that is hard to credit. Freemasonry's own rituals, mythology, and traditions, on the other hand, indicate a far more venerable birth in Biblical Israel, with the building of Solomon's Temple, and Ancient Egypt. Yet another origin has been suggested that manifests a high degree of credibility: namely, that it sprang from the guilds of Craftmasons of the medieval era.

What is the true nature of Freemasonry? Is it an evil or dangerous vehicle of power and corruption, or an organization that, teaching through allegory and ritual, strives to "make good men better"? What is the truth about this controversial organization's origins, its aims, and its place in society today? The innate secrecy that has shrouded the fraternity since it first came to public notice poses incredible difficulties to any non-mason reflecting on these important issues.

The controversies that have dogged the Freemasons, and the mystery surrounding their spiritual ancestors, the Knights Templar, have tended to detract from the fact that their common knowledge and insight form what can be considered the single most important continuous strand in the entire Western esoteric tradition. This tradition—which, despite its hidden nature, was described by Professor Theodore Roszak of California State University as "probably the single, most profoundly imaginative and influential spiritual tradition of European culture"—exerted a seminal influence on the thinking of the builders of the great cathedrals, on leading teachers in ecclesiastical schools, on philosophers, playwrights, and poets such as Shakespeare, Goethe, Blake, and W. B. Yeats, on artists and Renaissance giants such as Leonardo da Vinci and Michelangelo, and indirectly on European Christendom for nearly 2,000 years. It is also the root from which sprang alchemy and modern science.

While there has been enough continuity to use the term "tradition" accurately, it should, nonetheless, be understood as one that is dynamic, pervasive, loose, and constantly re-synthesizing, disappearing from plain sight for most of the time, only to be intermittently and indirectly perceived by its fruits. This vital tradition does indeed have its origins in the mystical teachings of Biblical Israel and Ancient Egypt. These flourished openly in Ancient Greece and the tolerant Roman Empire but were forced to go underground in order to survive the regime of repression that was imposed on emerging Christian Europe.

As I noted at the beginning of this introduction, the very mention of Freemasonry can provoke strong responses. It is possible that some of the views expressed in this book will do so, too. Here, I follow a line of argument shared by many others (you will find some of these in the bibliography), but one which does not, nevertheless, fall within "mainstream" thinking. As a Freemason, I have studied this subject in depth for many years and have come to the conclusions that you will find in this book.

A MEDIEVAL VIEW OF THE BUILDING OF SOLOMON'S TEMPLE IN JERUSALEM. WAS THIS THE BIRTHPLACE OF FREEMASONRY?

the cradle of culture

The culture of classical Greece spawned one of the most dramatic and transformative eras in history: one that nurtured the seeds of our own modern culture. In that seminal age, the shores of the Mediterranean were the site of an exceptional concurrence of peoples and cultures whose religious and philosophical development were a unique blend of spiritual and material thinking which, allied to reason, form the very basis of modern scientific thought.

The foundation for this massive and sustained outpouring of intellectual and artistic activity was the "hidden stream of Gnostic thought" that the Greeks inherited from Ancient Egypt, refined, and developed. This was enshrined in the beliefs of the secret "mystery" cults—beliefs that ran through that culture like a river nourishing all in its path, sustaining the first dramatic flowering of European culture; of art, architecture, philosophy, drama, oratory, politics, medicine, and science in Ancient Greece. Above all, it was logic that came into its own, a form of thinking that was to dominate Western thought past the dawn of the Renaissance and up to the modern scientific age.

OPPOSITE: THE ACROPOLIS IN
ATHENS, AN OUTSTANDING
EXAMPLE OF CLASSICAL GREEK
SACRED ARCHITECTURE.

LEFT: THE MODERN IDEAL OF
BEAUTY, THE GREEK SCULPTURE
OF VENUS DE MILO.

*The rise of Greek civilization which produced this
outburst of intellectual activity is one of the most
spectacular events in history. Nothing like it has
ever occurred before or since. Within the short
space of two centuries, the Greeks poured forth
in art, literature, science, and philosophy an
astonishing stream of masterpieces which have
set the general standards of Western civilization.
Philosophy and science begin with Thales of
Miletus in the early sixth century BC.*
Bertrand Russell,

The Wisdom of the West

There was no doubt in the Greek mind
that thinking was concerned with sacred
knowledge and mystical insight, the vision of
which was as real to his humankind as the substance of the
phenomenal, physical world. In the Gnostic's view, thinking,
alone and unaided, could attain to "the good, the beautiful,
and the true."

THE ANCIENT FOUNDATIONS OF MODERN CULTURE

Throughout history, the speed of development of differing
cultures varied from community to community, depending
on the quality of the spiritual insights that fueled their drive
toward civilization. Evidence, scanty though it may be,
demonstrates that our Neolithic ancestors in Europe had a
profound reverence for "mother earth," for plants and
animals, for the very elements themselves. In time, mother
earth took on new names and was married in mythology
with the stars or the sky. New, lesser gods emerged,

replacing the spirits who had previously been
believed to inhabit different plants and animals,
until by the early years of classical Greece a
complex pantheon of gods was believed to
exist on the heavenly abode of Mount
Olympus, with Zeus rising above them
all. These gods were held to be capricious,
mischievous, and in conflict with each other,
treating men as mere pawns as if in some
complex, irrational, heavenly chess game.
With increasing influence from the
empires of the east, another important
trend developed in a new and
significantly different way, the
effects of which were to indirectly,
but completely, change the world.
The importation of initiation cults and their development
into the "hidden mysteries," or hermetic cults, created the
fertile seedbed for the flowering of philosophy, science,
art, and architecture.

All the "hidden mysteries" have a common origin. The
English author Colin Wilson writes of "the few"—the natural
leaders of every tribe or community—who knew of their
innate spiritual powers and deliberately sought means of
extending and strengthening them. The mystery cults of
early man arose when "the few" tried to gain knowledge
of the three inescapable facts of life that confront all
mankind: toil, pain, and death. The original path of initiation
arose from the latter view in which toil, pain, and death
were regarded as the means through which humanity was
protected from evil.

THE STEPPED PYRAMID OF ZOSER
IN CAIRO, DESIGNED BY THE
PRIEST/ARCHITECT IMHOTEP.

MYSTERY CULTS IN EGYPT AND GREECE

In Egypt and later in Greece, initiation into the temple
mysteries was restricted to a privileged few. The sacred
knowledge imparted as a result of initiation sustained the
Egyptian empire for over 2,000 years and attained levels of
incredible sophistication in art, architecture, astronomy,
medicine, and science. Initiation rites and the ceremonies of
the mystery cults were secret. The participants were
granted knowledge of the spiritual world during the ecstatic
periods of these rituals, which were held to be so sacred
that they could not be revealed to outsiders except on pain
of death. However, the sacred knowledge, or Gnosis,
imparted as the result of these rites, although granted to the
privileged few, was used for the benefit of the entire nation.
Some of the Greek cults, just like the Essenes of Israel,
developed a deep cosmology and, oddly enough,
characteristics that were replicated in the early years of
Christian belief and practice. These usually included some
form of baptism by fire or water, the confession of sins, a
period of purification and fasting, and a ritual meal of bread
and water or wine. All of which were, in one form or
another, part of the initiation rites.

INITIATORY CULTS AND ORDERS

ASSOCIATIONS AND GROUPINGS IN WHICH BENEFITS ARE OBTAINED
OR PROGRESS IS MADE ONLY BY VIRTUE OF BEING A MEMBER,
WHETHER SECRET OR PUBLIC.

Two of the earliest and perhaps the purest of such
mystery cults were the Magi of Persia and the Orphic cults
in Greece. The Orphic mystery religion was believed to have
been founded by the legendary singer Orpheus, an
approximate contemporary of Zoroaster. Its doctrine tends
toward asceticism and emphasizes mental ecstasy. By this it
was hoped to achieve "enthusiasm" (entheoism—or god
within) and as a result gain mystical knowledge.

These initiation cults each had a library of sacred texts
and held their followers together by bonds of shared belief.
This gave rise to a body of philosophy that was directly
related to real life and the temporal world, and which
provided just the vibrant conception that was needed for a
passionate search for truth and beauty. Each cult or mystery
school clung closely to the well-established links between
the divine and the earthly. A close study of the Isis cult from
Egypt reinforces these close links between the teaching of
the mystery schools and the cycles of growth and
regeneration of the earth in all its fruitfulness.

GREEK GNOSTIC PHILOSOPHY

The supposed author of the earliest mystery texts that are
still extant is Hermes Trismegistos, usually identified with
the divine Hermes, the messenger of the gods, or equated
with the Egyptian god Thoth who was also the scribe of the
gods. These texts only came to light in the third century of
the Christian era. It is now generally accepted that the
contents of the texts themselves, or at least of such
fragments as have survived, are authentic and confirm the
link between Greek Hermetic schools and the mystery cults
of Ancient Egypt. This is reinforced when we identify the first

verifiable Greek initiate who can clearly be seen to be an historical figure—a supreme individual who exerted a formative and important influence on Greek thought, science and philosophy; a mathematician, the founder of a school, and a religious mystic who was interested in everything—Pythagoras. Pythagoras is often associated with the Persian Magi and with the Chaldeans, and he is reported to have spent ten years in Babylon studying the Mesopotamian mysteries. According to Posidonius, one of Pythagoras's principal teachers was Abaris the Druid, who came from Scotland. Having returned briefly to Greece, Pythagoras founded a school in Crotona in southern Italy, which soon acquired a glowing reputation that ensured its survival for over 30 years. This was a school for mystics whose initiation rites were both lengthy and rigorous, and it was here that he developed his philosophy—a brand of philosophy that became, over the centuries, one of the most profound and lasting influences over the entire field of mysticism and the occult.

Under the influence of the Pythagoreans, the old Olympian religion began to be displaced and a new, distinctly spiritual outlook took its place.

The outpouring of art, philosophy, and literature that accompanied and sustained the emergence of Greek civilization eventually, by a rather tortuous route, passed down to us virtually intact. The works of Pythagoras, Socrates, and Plato are the foundation of all our mathematics and philosophy. Greek culture quickly developed all of the literary forms that we now regard as classic. Experience, knowledge, inquiry, and expectations—all were recorded and passed on.

CARVING OF PYTHAGORAS ON THE SOUTH PORCH OF THE WEST FRONT OF CHARTRES CATHEDERAL.

ABOVE: A STATUE OF THE PHILOSOPHER SOCRATES, WHO BELIEVED THAT IGNORANCE WAS THE CAUSE OF SIN.

RIGHT: MAP OF THE ROMAN EMPIRE, WHICH SPREAD FROM BRITAIN IN THE WEST TO ASSYRIA IN THE EAST, AND ENCOMPASSED THE ENTIRE MEDITERRANEAN COAST.

This irreversible accumulation, the very art of storage and transmission of ideas and experience, constantly both augmented consciousness and acted as a catalyst for further evolution: an evolution which, in turn, eventually transformed human life itself.

THE GOOD, THE BEAUTIFUL, AND THE TRUE

The power and cumulative influence of the Gnostic initiatory culture that developed in Ancient Greece influenced all the cultures that followed for over two millennia, including many of the so-called modern advances of the twentieth and twenty-first centuries. The new philosophy held that thought, philosophy, and politics would inevitably lead to the knowledge of "the good, the beautiful, and the true," and that law, man-made terrestrial law, was the ultimate expression of this. Law was given the twin accords of respect and a capacity for ultimate perfection as the expression of the state, and therefore also of man.

IERVSALEM   VENICE   CONSTANTINOPLE   ALEXANDRIA   ETERNALL CITY TO ROMVLVS AVTHOTOR

A NEW MAPPE OF THE ROMANE EMPIRE

newly described by Iohn Speede and are
to be sold by Tho: Bassett in Fleet street,
& Ric: Chiswell in St Pauls Churchyard.

NORTH

The German ocean

Frisij

GERMANIE

GETAE.

THE LAND OF SARMATIA.

Colchis

Pannonia

NORI CVM

DACIA

MYSIA

Thra cia

THE EUXINE SEA

IBE RIA

ALBA NIA

THE CASPIAN SEA OR HIRCIAN

MEDIA

ASSY RIA.

A S I A

HEL ES

ARME NIAE

Mace

LYDIA

PAMPH ILIA

CILI CIA.

MESOPO TA MIA

The low Sea

The Sardinia Sea

Creta

Ciprus

SYRIA

BABI LON

Sinus Persicus

MIDDLE   LAND SEA

Sicilia

CYRENE.

AEGYPT

AFRICK THE LESSE

MARMARICA.

PART OF ARABIA

Parte of the Arabian Sea

ye Beginning Increase & Height of ye Romane Empire

for 243 yeares the Romane Empire came no further then unto ye haven & ye sacrifices with in ye
in there were sometymes Dictatovrs who pronounced things to others to be written & Decommitten
to ye warr for the space of 447 yeares until Italie beyond Padum was taken. Africk and
tributarias the Illyrians Histrians Libernians Dalmatians were tamed it passed forward to
ade warr with the Dardanians Moesians & Thracians it came unto Danubium & the Romanes
driven away. Methridates being overcome the Kyngdome of ye Sea was taken with Armenia
unto Mesopotamia & entred into Legnia wth ye Parthians made warr against ye Carduens Sara:
Cilicia & Syria being brought vnder their power at ye last it came vnto Egipt But vnder
to the times of Theodosius the chief & Honovius & Aradius his sones for the space of 440
came vnder ye yoake The Alpes of ye Sea & of Rhetia Norivum Pannonia & Moesia came
vas brought vnder into prouences all ye Sea & Armenia ye Greater Mesopotamia Assyria
Romane Empire thus by this meanes & by those principall men & by ye power of the
most noble empire was brough vnto ye topp of his hieght whose borders were towards ye West
East Tigeris from ye South mount Atlas all which things are sett in this table

HIS WYFE

A ITALIEN

HIS WYFE

A EGIPTIAN

HIS WYFE

The humility of Socrates was such that he held that he himself knew nothing, yet he believed that knowledge lay within the reach of all who earnestly sought it. He believed that sin derived from man's lack of knowledge, and that if only man had sufficient knowledge he would not sin. Thus the overriding cause of sin was ignorance. To reach "the Good," therefore, we must attain knowledge. The sacred and indissoluble link between "the Good" and knowledge became one of the hallmarks of Greek thought and philosophy for many centuries. The contrast between this philosophical concept and the dogmas of early Christianity could not be starker, for the medieval Christian ethic is quite opposed to the ideas of Socrates. Indeed, according to the British philosopher Bertrand Russell, the early popes, and all those who inherited their mantle for many centuries to come, held that the most important quality was a pure heart and a capacity for implicit belief, and that therefore these qualities were more likely to be found among the ignorant.

Flowering of art, literature, philosophy, and the new sciences took place during this truly seminal era. Yet how did the concepts of "the Good, the Beautiful, and the True" spread and ramify their undoubted influence throughout the known world, not only at that time but even down to the present day? To answer this question we must turn our attention to an empire established by military force and alliances that created a stability, power, and influence that the Greeks themselves, for all their achievements, never attained. An empire based on concepts of order and stability never sustained before, or for so long, over such a wide area, which provided the perfect vehicle for the transmission of ideas—the Empire of Rome.

MYSTERY CULTS IN THE ROMAN EMPIRE

Rome took to its very heart the full flowering of the first fruits of Greek Hermetic consciousness and spread them throughout the world. Thus it was the combination of two distinct and separate national characteristics—firstly that of the sublimely gifted, inspired creators and innovators, the Greeks and secondly, the sharp-eyed innovative, pragmatic, and powerful Romans—that developed the political and intellectual climate within which were refined the ideas that became the very foundation and the cornerstone of Western culture for the two millennia that followed.

By the time of the birth of Jesus, the Roman Empire, which had doubled in size every generation since its foundation, encompassed nearly all the then known world. It comprised virtually the entire Mediterranean littoral and had pushed its borders well beyond—westward into Spain, France, and Britain, and then northward into Germany. Although imposed by force, it was in many ways a liberal empire, for having gained territory by force, it maintained its rule by military might twinned with tolerant acceptance of local customs and religions—as long as the Roman law was upheld and lip service given to the state religion. Thus for the first time there arose an imperial establishment that brought stability, widespread peace, freedom of movement and trade, all allied to tolerance for old religious forms, local customs, and new philosophical ideas. Ideas were far from regimented and stultified; indeed, their propagation and exchange were actively encouraged. Thus Rome absorbed the art, philosophy, and religious culture that was the glory of Greece, raised it to a pinnacle of respect, and then became the means whereby Greek culture, religion, and ideas were transmitted throughout the world.

Mystery cults began to infiltrate Roman life during the Republic. Some cults took root in their original form; others became modified with the latinization of the original Greek names, or the identification of Greek gods with specifically Roman deities. Certain cults eventually degenerated into social clubs for men only, and few of the truly great initiation cults lasted for long, with the notable exceptions of the Persian cult of Mithras and the Egyptian cult of Isis. In the two centuries following the birth of Jesus, the Mithraic cult of solar worship under the protection of the god Sol Invictus grew in popularity. Knowledge of the various gods and their cults spread widely, providing a confusing multiplicity of religious ideas which, as often as not, intermingled, spawning new ones all the time.

Transcending all religions and ideas of tribe or nationality, and rising above them all, was the respect accorded to education—the perfect vehicle for the new philosophical and spiritual ideas from Greece. Theology was inseparable from philosophy. Had not the first philosophers of note been initiates into the spiritual worlds? Rhetoric became the handmaiden of both; Greek the common language of the educated empire. Thus religion, through its main derivative philosophy, became the guide to intimate personal conduct, responsibility, and moral virtue and, as a consequence of the Greek Hermetic and philosophical influence, an age of personal religion dawned that stood in stark contrast to the collective state or tribal religions of the recent past.

FAR LEFT: CARVINGS OF ISIS AND HORUS ON AN EGYPTIAN TEMPLE WALL.

BELOW: STATUES OF A GREEK GOD AND GODDESS.

Greek culture in this way provided an ambience within which the intellect was used to transform religious ideas, but they were all ideas that came from other cultures and other times—Babylon, Persia, Egypt—and were now re-synthesized in Greek forms. The Greek cosmology, such as it was, derived directly from these ancient sources, as we have seen in the case of Pythagoras and those who followed him. Building on this foundation, the Roman Empire created and sustained a world of religious tolerance, high levels of culture and art, and a deep respect for the values of education. The only exceptions to the rule of religious tolerance arose in the treatment meted out by Rome to the Druids of Celtic Culture and to the emerging Christian religion.

ISIS CULT

THE CULT OF THE EGYPTIAN GODDESS ISIS WAS ORIGINALLY BASED ON FERTILITY RITES THAT, BY LATE ROMAN TIMES, HAD BECOME IMMORAL; NONETHELESS, THE IMAGE OF ISIS WITH HER SON HORUS SEEMED TO EARLY ROMAN CHRISTIANS TO REFLECT THE IMAGE OF THE VIRGIN MARY WITH JESUS AND MAY ACCOUNT FOR SOME OCCURRENCES OF THE BLACK MADONNA.

the birth of christianity

EVANGELISM, THE DEIFICATION OF JESUS, DISPUTE, DISUNITY, AND THE RISE OF A REPRESSIVE SOCIETY WERE THE HALLMARKS OF THE FIRST FOUR HUNDRED YEARS OF CHRISTIANITY.

The Romans destroyed Druidic culture in both Gaul and Britain simply because the Druids were acting as the focus for resistance against the Empire. The intermittent persecution of the Christians started as the result of the whim of the deranged Emperor Nero, and while sometimes repeated by others, was rare, intermittent, and in the later years, mainly punitively financial in nature.

Christianity, at that time, was very different from the religion we know today. It was a scattered collection of small congregations all claiming to follow the teachings of Jesus the Nazorean, the leader of an offshoot of the Essenes, who had been crucified for sedition in Jerusalem *circa* 33 CE. After his death the movement carried on under the leadership of Jesus' brother James the Just, the first so-called "bishop" of Jerusalem. James and the original disciples did not believe that Jesus had founded a new religion and continued their daily attendance at the temple. For them, the teachings of Jesus were in total conformity with the Jewish mysticism of both the *merkabah* or *hekaloth* traditions, and used a transformational form of initiation to purify its members so that they might inspire brotherhood and justice among men. Jesus was regarded as a divinely inspired teacher whose objective was to "create an elite within the elite" that would purify the people of Israel who would then become "a light to all nations."

Yet despite the clear evidence that proves that James was the true leader of Jesus' disciples after the Crucifixion, neither he nor the Church's prime candidate St. Peter is known as "the Father of Christianity"—that title is instead bestowed on Saul of Tarsus, otherwise known as St. Paul who, according to his own accounts at least, never met

SAUL OF TARSUS, OTHERWISE KNOWN AS ST. PAUL, THE AUTHOR OF THE EARLIEST CHRISTIAN DOCUMENTS AND THE FIRST APOSTLE TO DESCRIBE JESUS AS GOD.

JAMES THE JUST, THE BROTHER OF
JESUS AND, ACCORDING TO THE ACTS
OF THE APOSTLES, THE FIRST BISHOP
OF JERUSALEM.

Jesus. Paul's epistles confirm that he was a member of the Herodian royal family, well connected with the Roman Imperial household, a Roman citizen, and a Pharisee who spent some time persecuting the followers of Jesus after the Crucifixion. After his miraculous conversion on the road to Damascus he changed his name, and then joined James in Jerusalem to learn the "true Way" as taught by Jesus, before setting out on a series of prolonged evangelical journeys.

CONFLICT BETWEEN JAMES AND PAUL

It may come as a surprise to many Christians today to learn that within a remarkably short time Paul was subject to bitter criticism and was vehemently rejected by James and the original disciples in Jerusalem, for there was a major and fundamental difference between the Way, as interpreted by James and his Essene companions (who after the Crucifixion became known as the Ebionites or "the Poor") and the version preached by Paul. James and the Ebionites had an absolute dedication to the Torah, maintained a strict prohibition against mixing with gentiles and kept strictly to the dietary laws of Judaism. This strict interpretation was diametrically opposed by Paul who mixed freely with gentiles and preached that the Torah no longer applied. Furthermore, it was Paul who first made the blasphemous claim that Jesus was divine and had died to save us from sin. As a result, Paul was expelled from the community and even his closest associate Barnabas deserted him. The devout Catholic historian Paul Johnson wrote that from this time onward the evangelical mission of St. Paul steadily lost ground to that of the evangelists duly accredited by James the Just in Jerusalem.

James and the disciples regarded Paul as a false prophet. Iraneus, Bishop of Lyon, quotes an Ebionite document that describes Paul as "an apostate of the Law." Another Ebionite document, the *Kerygmata Petrou*, described Paul as "an apostate of the Law," or a "spouter of wickedness and lies" and "the distorter of the true teachings of Jesus." Thus we can see that the family and disciples of Jesus viewed Paul with considerable contempt, and Paul's epistles disclose that these feelings were mutual. Paul Johnson claims that if it was not for the death of James the Just and the destruction of Jerusalem by the Romans in 70 CE, the Pauline doctrine of the divinity of Jesus would have vanished without trace. After the fall of Jerusalem and the destruction of the Temple, the teachings of Paul—that Jesus was God incarnate and had died to save us from sin—slowly began to predominate. Meanwhile, the 24 families of the *ma'madot*, the hereditary high priest of the Temple of Jerusalem, scattered and fled. Among them were the surviving members of Jesus' own family, the Desposyni, who as descendants of the Royal House of David were part of that group. Many went to Europe; others went east across the River Jordan.

THE EMPEROR NERO, WHO PERSECUTED EARLY
CHRISTIAN COMMUNITIES IN ROME.

THE SPREAD OF PAULINE CHRISTIANITY

The Christians who accepted the doctrines devised by St. Paul had congregations at Ephesus, Corinth, and in Rome itself. It was this branch of emerging Christianity who bore the main brunt of the persecution initiated by the Emperor Nero, who used this community as scapegoats blamed for starting the Great Fire in Rome. Many were martyred in the Coliseum. However, persecution of this new religious sect was sporadic, infrequent, and—apart from isolated cases of individual execution, such as that of St. Mauritius, for example—usually was restricted to fines, loss of property, and disbarment from public office. The reasons for this growing toleration are not hard to find, for in his epistles Paul had stressed the duty that bound all Christians—to obey lawful authorities. This made for subservient and law-abiding congregations. Indeed, the persecutions that did take place after the death of Nero were almost solely directed at individuals who had refused to publicly honor the traditional gods of Rome. However, time did not heal the

divisions among the Christians. They were still bitterly divided between those who believed that Jesus had come to reveal a Gnostic, fundamentally Jewish pathway to initiation, and those who believed that he was God who had come to Earth to redeem mankind from sin.

As the Pauline theologians strove to tighten their grip over the emerging "Christian Church" they used calumny and falsehood to devalue the views of their opponents. The tone of these debates was such that it became known as *odium theologicum*, a form of slander and abuse directed not at the intellectual or spiritual content of their opponents' viewpoint, but at the personal character and alleged habits of those that disagreed with them. However, it was not the quality of debate that ensured the rise to absolute power of the Pauline theologians; it was the earthly ambitions and political skill of a pagan general who became Emperor of Rome. Constantine the great settled matters once and for all. Constantine fought a bitter civil war for power and won the Battle of the Milvian Bridge in 312 CE to become Emperor. A follower of the Mithraic cult of Sol Invictus, he was the son of a Christian mother who sought to use the

ST. PAUL (PAUL OF TARSUS)

SELF-APPOINTED CHRISTIAN APOSTLE WHOSE IDEAS AND METHODS TRANSFORMED THE JEWISH-ORIENTED BELIEFS AND RITES OF EARLY CHRISTIANITY INTO THE "OPEN" CHURCH IT HAS BEEN NOW FOR MILLENNIA; PAUL HIMSELF WAS A WELL-EDUCATED ROMAN CITIZEN WITH FRIENDS (AND PROBABLY RELATIONS) IN HIGH PLACES; IT WAS HE AND HIS GREEK-SPEAKING ASSOCIATES WHO INSURED THE DOCUMENTATION OF HIS VERSION OF CHRISTIANITY.

disciplined law-abiding traditions of the Christians as a socially cohesive force to heal the bitter divisions created by the recent civil war.

THE COUNCIL OF NICEA

It was after assuming power, when Constantine made Christianity a *religio licta*, or an approved religion, that matters came to a head. The council of Nicea in 325 CE was convened by Constantine to end the bitter controversy over the nature of Jesus, to buttress the power of the clergy, and to condemn heresy in all its forms. In reality it gave the Church a power base that it has used, enlarged, and exploited ever since. However, as a means of ending disputes it was a failure. After the Council of Nicea Constantine made it clear that the benefits he had granted to the Christian Church "must benefit only adherents of the Catholic Faith"—a faith defined in the terms of those who accepted the Pauline doctrine without reservation and who accepted the supreme ecclesiastical authority of the Bishop of Rome. He stated: "Heretics and Schismatics shall not only be alien from these privileges but shall be bound and subjected to various public services." The emperors who followed continued the same policy, and membership of "heretical" sects incurred a degree of infamy and a loss of civil rights. The first specific laws against heresy were promulgated in the 380s, and by the time of Emperor Theodosius in the fifth century, had multiplied until there were over 100 statutes aimed at heretics. Dissent was thus forced to go underground, especially after Priscillian of Avila was burned alive for heresy in 383 CE.

CONSTANTINE THE GREAT. A WORSHIPER OF THE MITHRAIC CULT OF SOL INVICTUS, HE ALLOWED CHRISTIANITY TO BECOME A STATE-LICENSED RELIGION.

THE PRIMACY OF THE BISHOP OF ROME

The power and authority of the Bishop of Rome over the Christian world was now increasing exponentially. James the Just, as high priest at the temple in Jerusalem, had acted as the representative of his people before God, pleading for forgiveness of sin. Now, the Bishop of Rome, or Pope as he was soon to be called, claimed to be the representative of God before the people, divinely ordained with spiritual

underground to ensure their survival. Scattered throughout Europe, Arabia, Egypt, and the Near East, they learned to dissemble in order to survive. Outwardly they followed the prevailing religion of their place and time; in secret they preserved the true initiatory teachings of Jesus and spread the fruits of their Gnostic insight to benefit the communities within which they moved. According to this theory, henceforth they referred to themselves as

authority that far exceeded that granted to other bishops, kings or emperors. Faced with the absolute power of the new Church/State establishment, the members of the Ebionites and the descendants of the 24 high-priestly families of the *ma'madot* living in the Empire went

Rex Deus or, more simply "the Families."

The increasingly powerful Church was universally and absolutely intolerant of all rivals and swept away all other sources of knowledge of the spiritual world. It campaigned vigorously throughout the Empire for the destruction or

RIGHT: POPE LEO III CROWNING CHARLEMAGNE AS THE FIRST HOLY ROMAN EMPEROR.

RIGHT: POPE LEO III CROWNING CHARLEMAGNE AS THE FIRST HOLY ROMAN EMPEROR.

BELOW: THE CHURCH CAMPAIGNED VIGOROUSLY FOR THE DESTRUCTION OR CLOSURE OF ALL PAGAN TEMPLES.

closure of all the temples and centers of worship of rival faiths, wherever possible hijacking these sacred sites for its own use. The Greek mystery temples were rendered defunct and the oracle of Delphi was silenced for all time. The Church in its deliberate march toward absolute power and authority denied all access to the realms of either sacred or secular knowledge that it did not control. Who knows what might happen if people were encouraged into education, intellectual adventure, and inquiry? Education was therefore restricted to the clergy, and holy orders became the essential prerequisite for basic literacy. Thus during the Dark Ages in Europe, outside the ranks of the clergy, nobles, kings, and emperors were nearly all illiterate, as were the common people.

CHARLEMAGNE

Charles the Great, better known as Charlemagne, could hardly write his own name. Nonetheless he was crowned and anointed as the new Holy Roman Emperor by Pope Leo III in 800 CE. One historian of the Carolingian era, P. Munz, writing long before any disclosure of the Rex Deus traditions, asserted that Charlemagne claimed succession from the Biblical kings of Israel and was, therefore, a member of the Rex Deus group of families. Eventually he ruled over a territory that reached from the Danube to the Mediterranean and made forays into Moorish Spain, unsuccessful in the north but capturing the important areas known as the Spanish Marches in the south. Charlemagne created over 600 counties that enabled his orders to be implemented with considerable efficiency by his appointees the counts, themselves often members of the Rex Deus family group—especially in the regions of greatest potential danger, the borderlands of Islamic Spain. And so by the time of Charlemagne's death in 814, much of Europe—particularly France, Septimania, Provence, northern Italy and Saxony— was administered by the Rex Deus nobility. A nobility imbued with absolute loyalty to Charlemagne, they were heretics to a man, who passed down the hidden teachings of Jesus in secret within their family groups, but who, in order to survive, outwardly practiced Christianity.

hidden streams of spirituality

HERESY FLOURISHED SECRETLY DESPITE THE APPARENT REPRESSIVE DEGREE OF CONTROL EXERCISED BY THE CHURCH, AND HERETICAL SECRET TEACHINGS EXERTED A DEGREE OF INFLUENCE BOTH WITHIN THE CHURCH AND AMONG THE LAITY.

several branches of the Rex Deus families had sought refuge in parts of Europe that lay far beyond even the boundaries of Charlemagne's expanded empire, and were thus well out of reach of the ever-growing tentacles of Holy Mother the Church. Within Christian Europe, the families included, among many others: the eleventh-century Saxon Royal house of England; the Capetian Royal House of France, who claimed descent from Mary Magdalene; the St. Clairs of Roslin in Scotland; the ducal House of Burgundy; the aristocratic families of Chaumont, Gisors, d'Evreux and Blois, the family of the Counts of Champagne, and the Royal House of Flanders.

When we study the genealogies of these families, we find that they made repeated marital alliances with each other, time after time, for all these marriages were conducted from within a select group and the same names appear in the genealogies of all of them, every third or fourth generation. The explanation for these seemingly incestuous marital alliances is that the Rex Deus group, just like the Cohens of Biblical Israel from whom they all claimed descent, were not allowed to marry outside their own small, select group.

Knights from 11 leading Scottish Rex Deus families accompanied Henri de St. Clair of Roslin when he went to the Holy Land with Geoffroi de Bouillion on the First Crusade in 1096 and were all present at the capture of Jerusalem. This group included ancestors of the Stuarts, the Montgomerys, Setons, Douglases, Dalhousies, Ramseys, Leslies, and Lindsays—all families linked by marriage, shared heretical beliefs, and a common ancestry that reached back in time through Biblical Israel to Ancient Egypt. Representatives of Rex Deus were thus reaching for positions of power and influence throughout Christian Europe.

THE KNIGHTS TEMPLAR AND THE CISTERCIANS

The Rex Deus families extended their influence throughout the European nobility and also began to spread their tentacles into the organization of its main opponent—namely the Church—by acts of protection to various churches and cathedrals. Some members joined the Church itself and attempted to influence their corrupt enemy from within. Events within one family illustrate some of the tensions this strategy could provoke.

Bernard de Fontaine, later canonized as St. Bernard of Clairvaux, expressed a wish to join the struggling Cistercian Order, and his family were horrified—yet their attitude was soon transformed, for reasons that are still far from clear. Opposition to his plans did not merely evaporate but, stranger still, a large number of his male relatives and friends chose to follow him into the Order: no fewer than 32 of them became novices with Bernard when he joined the Order in 1112.

Bernard attained an almost unbelievable position of power with inexplicable speed, becoming the principal personal advisor to two popes who had been his pupils. He also exerted considerable influence over temporal affairs, becoming an advisor to kings, emperors, and the nobility. His Rex Deus connections were the essential key to attaining this commanding position. His commitment to initiatory teaching is demonstrated by the 120 sermons that he preached based on the *Song of Songs* by King Solomon and he extended this form of teaching by acting as the spiritual advisor to a branch of the Compagnonnage, or Craftmasons, known as the Children of Solomon. However, Bernard also conspired with other members of the Rex Deus to achieve one objective that left an indelible mark on the course of European history. His fellow conspirators included his cousin, who later became patriarch of Jerusalem; his uncle André de Montbard; Hughes de Payen; the St. Clairs of Roslin; the Setons; the Royal House of Flanders; and one of the leading noblemen in Europe at that time, Count Hughes of Champagne.

THE COUNTS OF CHAMPAGNE

The Counts of Champagne were members of Rex Deus who were linked both by blood and marriage to the St. Clairs, the Capetian kings of France, the Duke of Burgundy, the Duke of Normandy, and the Norman and Plantagenet Kings of England. Hughes' seat of power, the city of Troyes in the county of Champagne, became a center of learning that attracted scholars and intellectuals of repute. Several Jewish families settled in Troyes and one produced a son who

became, arguably, the greatest Jewish Biblical scholars of all time, Rabbi Solomon ben Isaac, known as Rachi. As a philosopher, he is considered second only to the incomparable Moses Maimonides. Rachi also maintained a school of considerable stature in the city, which was devoted to the study of the Kabbala, the principal spiritual pathway of Hebraic and Ancient Egyptian initiation.

In 1104, Hughes I de Champagne met secretly with the members of the Rex Deus families of Brienne, de Joinville,

RIGHT: TEMPLAR SEAL OF THE TEMPLE OF SOLOMON.

LEFT: ST. BERNARD OF CLAIRVAUX (C.1090–1153). BERNARD WAS A CLERIC OF IMMENSE ENERGY WHO ESTABLISHED ALMOST 70 HOUSES FOR THE CISTERCIANS.

Chaumont, and Anjou. Shortly afterward he left for the Holy Land and did not return to Champagne until 1108. In 1114 he made another brief and mysterious visit to Jerusalem, and on his return made a donation of land to the Cistercian Order upon which the monks built the Abbey of Clairvaux. Bernard de Fontaine was appointed its first abbot. These visits to the Holy Land and the donation of land to the Cistercians were the prologue to concerted action by Rex Deus that resulted in the foundation of an Order of warrior monks whose name was to resound through the annals of European history and cause considerable controversy right down to the present day—The Poor Knights of Christ and the Temple of Solomon, otherwise known as the Knights Templar.

THE KNIGHTS TEMPLAR

Bernard of Clairvaux rose to power not only because of his useful family connections but also as a result of his immense energy and superb intellect. He suffered from ill health throughout his life, yet he personally founded 68 Cistercian houses from his base at Clairvaux. An old and respected Provençal tradition recounts that Hughes of Champagne, Hughes de Payen, André de Montbard, and several of the other founding knights of the Templar Order visited the small church at Roquebillière in February 1117, stayed a few days, and then crossed the Alpes Maritimes by the Col de Turini to Seborga. This principality housed a Cistercian Abbey that was founded by Bernard of Clairvaux in 1113 to protect "a great secret." Under the direction of its abbot, Edouard, were two monks, Gondemar and Rossal. All three had joined the Order along with Bernard, and both Gondemar and Rossal had been knights before they became

monks. A document in the Seborga archives records that in February 1117, Bernard came to the abbey with seven companions, released Gondemar and Rossal from their vows, and gave a solemn blessing to the whole group which departed for Jerusalem in 1118. The document also states that prior to their departure, Bernard nominated Hughes de Payen as the Grand Master of "the Poor Militia of Christ," and that he was consecrated in that rank by Abbot Edouard.

THE FOUNDATION OF THE ORDER

An account by Guillaume de Tyre, however, written over 70 years after the event, places the foundation of the Order of the Knights Templar in Jerusalem in 1118. They were granted quarters on the Temple Mount by King Baldwin II, took the name of the "Poor Fellow-Soldiers of Jesus Christ" and were recognized as "the Knighthood of the Temple of Solomon." According to William of Tyre, the founding members were Hughes de Payen, its first Grand Master, André de Montbard, Geoffroi de St. Omer, Payen de Montdidier, Achambaud de St. Amand, Geoffroi Bisol, Godfroi, Gondemar, and Rossal. These Rex Deus knights were a tightly knit group of relatives who were closely associated with Count Hughes I of Champagne, and it can be argued that this is further proof of the conspiracy that led to the founding of the Order. Furthermore, Hughes de Champagne returned to the Holy Land in 1125 and joined the Templars where he had to swear unquestioning obedience to his own vassal, Hughes de Payen, the Grand Master of the Order.

THE CROSS OF LORRAINE

ONE FORM OF THE CROIX PATTÉE

ANOTHER FORM OF THE CROIX PATTÉE

THE FOUNDING MEMBERS

Hughes de Payen, who was born in 1070 at the de Payen chateau on the banks of the Seine, was the cousin of two of Europe's most powerful men, Bernard of Clairvaux and the Count of Champagne, who was also his overlord. He was known as "Hughes the Moor" because of his lineal descent from the Prophet Muhammad through the matrilineal line. André de Montbard was not only the uncle of Bernard of Clairvaux but also a kinsman of the Duke of Burgundy and yet another vassal of the house of Champagne. Geoffroi de St. Omer was the son of a leading Flemish nobleman, Hughes de St. Omer. Payen de Montdidier and Achambaud de St. Amand were both related to the Royal House of Flanders, whose sons Godfroi de Bouillion and Baudouin of Brittany, became rulers of the kingdom of Jerusalem; Godfroi as protector of the Holy Sepulchre, and after his death, Baudouin as King Baldwin I.

RECOGNITION OF THE ORDER

The Knights Templar received recognition from the Patriarch of Jerusalem, yet another distant cousin of Bernard of

PATRIARCH OF JERUSALEM

ORIGINALLY, THE LEADER OF THE EARLY CHRISTIAN COMMUNITY IN JERUSALEM, BUT IN RECENT CENTURIES COMPLICATED BY THE NUMBER OF DIFFERENT NATIONAL CHURCHES AND DENOMINATIONS CLAIMING TO BE BASED IN THE CITY; THE ROMAN CATHOLIC ARCHBISHOP OF JERUSALEM IS ENTITLED TO BE CALLED THE PATRIARCH, ALTHOUGH IN THE EYES OF MOST CHRISTIANS THE PATRIARCH OF JERUSALEM IS IN FACT THE LEADER THERE OF THE EASTERN ORTHODOX CHURCH; A THIRD SUCH IS THE ARMENIAN PATRIARCH OF JERUSALEM, LEADER OF THE ARMENIAN APOSTOLIC CHURCH.

Clairvaux, at the Council of Nablus in 1120 when he granted them their first insignia, a red two-barred cross that later became known as the Cross of Lorraine, it was only later that they used the various forms of the Croix Patté. The stated intention of the new Order was to protect pilgrims *en route* from the port of Jaffa to Jerusalem. Yet as Hughes de Payen was 48 years old at the time of the Order's foundation, and because most of his companions were of similar age, it is hard to imagine quite how they could possibly accomplish this mammoth task. The fact is that, far from patrolling the bandit-infested roads between the coast and Jerusalem, they spent the first nine years of the Order's existence excavating beneath the Temple Mount directly under their headquarters. During the later years of the nineteenth and the early years of the twentieth centuries, Lieutenant Warren of the Royal Engineers excavated the 80-foot vertical shaft that they dug and the system of radiating tunnels to which it led. Warren discovered a variety of Templar artifacts including a spur, the remains of a lance, a small Templar cross, and the major part of a Templar sword. In the light of the Rex Deus conspiracy that was afoot, several questions now arise. Was whatever they were seeking within these excavations the real reason that lay behind the founding of the Order? Precisely what were they seeking? How did they know where to dig? Lastly, how did they obtain quarters immediately above their chosen site of excavation?

One clue appears carved on a pillar in the Portal of the Initiates at Chartres Cathedral, which depicts the Ark of the Covenant being transported upon a wheeled cart. According to legend from Biblical times, the Ark of the Covenant was buried deep beneath the Temple in Jerusalem long before the Babylonian invasion. Another tradition claims that Hughes de Payen was chosen to retrieve it and bring it back to France, where it was at first hidden beneath the crypt of Chartres Cathedral. It has also been claimed that a vast quantity of ancient documents were discovered under the Temple, and a consensus has emerged that they probably contained, among other things, copies of the Dead Sea Scrolls as well as treatises on sacred geometry, ancient

of the Temple by the Romans in 70 CE. Many of the sites listed in the Copper Scroll were excavated by John Allegro, the Dead Sea Scrolls scholar, in which he found a considerable number of artifacts relating to the Templars, but not a thing from the first century CE.

The Rex Deus tradition explains these events by claiming that knowledge of these secret hiding places was passed down through the generations for over 1,000 years via the oral traditions of the families. The granting of quarters

A MEDIEVAL DEPICTION OF THE ARK OF THE COVENANT, WHICH LEGEND RECOUNTS WAS BUILT BY MOSES TO CARRY THE TABLETS OF STONE INSCRIBED WITH THE TEN COMMANDMENTS.

science, and other aspects of the Hebraic/Egyptian Gnostic tradition. Events following the translation of the Copper Scroll found at Qumran tend to confirm this theory. The Copper Scroll lists many sites where Temple treasure and items of sacred import were hidden prior to the destruction

directly above the treasure they sought demonstrates that King Baldwin was also part of the conspiracy, and it is interesting, to say the least, that the Order first "went public" within a few weeks of his accession whereas, by contrast, despite several visits to the Holy Land by both Hughes de Champagne and Hughes de Payen during the reigns of Godfroi de Bouillion and his brother Baldwin I, no attempt whatsoever had been made to found the Order.

THE RETURN TO EUROPE

King Baldwin II wrote to Bernard of Clairvaux requesting him to intercede with the pope for formal papal recognition of the Order, for Bernard was not only advisor to Pope Honorius II but also his former teacher. Hughes de Payen and his co-founders set sail for Provence and then traveled overland to Normandy, where he met the English King Stephen who gave him a *laissez-passer* allowing his party to travel through England and on to Scotland, where he stayed with the St. Clairs of Roslin.

King David of Scotland donated land to the new Order at Ballontrodoch that became the headquarters of the Order in Scotland and that has since been renamed Temple. This land adjoined the St. Clair estates so that communication between the St. Clairs and the Knights Templar could be discreetly maintained. These first donations of land had been long-planned and were soon followed by a veritable cascade of gifts of estates, castles, towns, farms, and villages throughout Christian Europe, and still more gifts of property and money followed the pope's official recognition of the Order and the award of its first "rule."

THE RULE OF THE TEMPLARS

Bernard of Clairvaux did indeed bring the Order to the attention of the pope, who commanded his papal legate in France, Cardinal Matthew d'Albano, to call a council of church and temporal dignitaries to legalize the new Order and give the knights their first religious rule. The Council opened at Troyes on January 14, 1128 under the direction of Cardinal d'Albano. On January 31, 1128, the Grand Master, Hughes de Payen, and his fellow knights were called to appear before the Council to receive the new "rule" that had been written by their co-conspirator, Bernard of Clairvaux. Later, in 1138, Pope Innocent II issued the papal bull *Omne datum optimum* that made the Templars responsible, through their Grand Master, to the pope and the pope alone. This freed the Templars from the authority of bishops, archbishops, kings, and emperors, and made it the most independent religious Order in the Christian world. It was soon to become the most powerful, both in wealth and military might.

GROWTH OF THE ORDER

Within three years of the Council of Troyes the Knights Templar had acquired land in Portugal, Spain, and Aragon. By the early 1140s, they had acquired enough land and had recruited sufficient members to sustain simultaneous military operations on two fronts, one in the Holy Land and the other against the Moors in Spain. In Europe and the Holy Land they became, in effect, the first full-time, professional standing army since the fall of the Roman Empire. The

AREAS OF REX DEUS INFLUENCE IN EUROPE: 11TH–15TH CENTURIES

❶	BARONY OF ROSLIN	⓫	BURGUNDY
❷	FLANDERS	⓬	PROVENCE
❸	NORMANDY	⓭	LOMBARDY AND TUSCANY
❹	BRITTANY	⓮	ENGLAND
❺	LA ROCHELLE	⓯	GALLICIA
❻	ANJOU	⓰	PORTUGAL
❼	GUYENNE	⓱	ARAGON
❽	LANGUEDOC	⓲	HOLY ROMAN EMPIRE
❾	CHAMPAGNE	⓳	MAJORCA
❿	BAR		

grants of land, castles, and other property came in so fast that, in some cases, the Order had to defer the establishment of garrisons in their new lands for several years due to a shortage of manpower. This situation arose because their main focus was always the protection of the Kingdom of Jerusalem. In the early years all who were capable of military service were immediately sent to the East with the utmost speed, following their Grand Master's example, for Hughes, accompanied by 300 knights drawn from the noblest families in Europe, had returned to the Holy Land in 1129. Bearing in mind the difficulties of communication within Europe in the early years of the twelfth century and the time it took to arm and equip these men and then transport them to the Holy Land, this massive influx of recruits is yet another example of long-term planning on a very large scale.

Bernard of Clairvaux wrote a tract *In Praise of the New Knighthood* that extolled the virtues of the Knights Templar and delineated the immense spiritual benefits that would accrue to those who supported its aims with acts of personal service, donations of land or money. Following its circulation, recruits and gifts of land and money flowed like a river at full flood straight into the arms of the Templars. They were not the only beneficiaries; the Cistercian Order also underwent an extraordinary period of expansion. In Bernard's lifetime they founded more than 300 new abbeys, the most rapid expansion of any monastic Order before or since. During Bernard's lifetime at least, the Cistercians and the Knights Templar were widely regarded as two arms of the same body: the contemplative monastic arm, and the strong, swift military arm.

France, Provence, the County of Champagne, Bar, England, Tuscany, and the area now known as the Languedoc/Roussillon became the major centers of Templar power, closely followed by Aragon, Galicia, Portugal, Scotland, Normandy, and the lands within the Holy Roman Empire. At the peak of their power their estates stretched from the Baltic to the Mediterranean and from the Atlantic

coastline to the Holy Land. The income from these vast holdings was devoted to maintaining their army and fortifications in the Holy Land. The Order left no stone unturned in its endeavor to maximize its profits and increase its efficiency and power.

The majority of Templar properties in Europe were not great castles but fortified farmhouses, mills, barns, small apsidal chapels, and commanderies or administrative centers. In the cities, strongholds were erected to act as secure places for treasure in transit or to hold troops *en route* to the Holy Land. The Order owned land in every climatic zone in Europe—farms, vineyards, pasturage for sheep and cattle, quarries, mines, mills, smithies, and stud farms—and thereby became, in effect, the first multinational conglomerate in history. The organizational skill required to

manage this enormous multi-faceted international enterprise and keep a standing army in the field at the same time was staggering. But they did it—and yet some of their critics within the modern Church dismiss them as "illiterates"! According to the US business consultant S. T. Bruno, the Templars managed their organization in a manner consistent with some of the most sophisticated and best management practices understood today in the twenty-first century.

LONG-DISTANCE TRADE

Prior to the foundation and establishment of the Templar Order in Europe, long-distance overland trade was fraught with difficulty, for barons imposed tolls on goods passing through their lands, and commodities and money in transit were easy meat for the many bandits who infested the countryside. The coming of the Templars changed all that, for their many estates gave them ideal bases to fulfill their primary function of protecting the pilgrimage routes. Long-distance travel and trade thus became safer, and large

regional markets began to appear and prosper, which further stimulated mercantile activity.

TEMPLAR BANKING

Trade of this nature cannot flourish for long without the financial infrastructure to sustain it, and the warrior monks now added another string to their bow. The knights were used to working in different currencies and organizing the safe transport of gold and money across Europe to finance their military activities in the Holy Land. Now they began to offer these financial services to the emerging trading classes and set themselves up as bankers, using a device they had learned from the Sufis of Islam, the "note of hand," to facilitate the transfer of funds from one part of Europe to another. They lent money to merchants, to popes, bishops, kings, emperors, nobles, and princes, with their financial

ABOVE: A TEMPLAR COMMANDERIE NEAR SEGOVIA IN SPAIN, SHOWING A COMPLEX OF BUILDINGS AND AN OCTAGONAL TEMPLAR CHURCH COMPLETE WITH TOWER AND ARSIDAL CHAPELS.

dealings backed by their reputation for probity, security, and accuracy. They rapidly became the wealthiest financial institution in the Christian world.

Travel and the transportation of goods could not take place in safety if the roads and trade routes were not effectively policed, and the Order of the Knights Templar certainly fulfilled that function and, as a consequence, played a significant role in creating the necessary conditions for the accumulation of capital. The political results that flowed from this commercial success resulted in a sustained and cumulative shift in the balance of power in Europe. Wealth and power began to move from the feudal barons to the emerging mercantile class in the towns and cities.

Their reputation for probity and their international nature allied to their military reputation led to leading Templars being appointed as ambassadors, advisors to kings, popes, and emperors, and to positions of responsibility in nearly every kingdom in which they operated. Templars thus rose to positions of almost incalculable power and influence throughout the European continent, in military matters, in diplomacy, in international politics and, above all, in the world of finance. This ultimately became the cause of their downfall. First, however, we should study certain other initiatory Orders with whom the Templars worked closely: the medieval Craftmasons.

LEFT: THE INTERIOR OF A ROUND TEMPLAR CHURCH BUILT ON THE PRINCIPLES OF OCTAGONAL SACRED GEOMETRY.

the medieval craftmasons

THE INITIATORY ORDERS OF THE CHILDREN OF FATHER SOUBISE, THE CHILDREN OF MAITRE JACQUES, AND THE CHILDREN OF SOLOMON, WHO CREATED MUCH OF THE ARCHITECTURAL LEGACY THAT STILL ADORNS THE EUROPEAN LANDSCAPE TODAY.

Robert Graves, who was not only a great poet and writer but also a mythologist of international repute, claimed that Freemasonry first began as a Sufi society that reached England in the guise of a craft guild during the reign of King Athelstan (ruled 924–939), and was then introduced into Scotland. He described the Sufic origins of the Craftmasons' guilds and the part played by Templar teaching and tradition in the transformation of these guilds into Freemasonry. Graves traced Sufi origins back to the second millennium BCE and recounted that their hidden wisdom was passed down the generations by a process of initiation, from master to pupil. He asserts that the role of the Sufi masters in the building of Solomon's Temple is a key point that is commemorated in Freemasonic ritual. The mystical founder and teacher of the Sufis, *el Khidir* was known as "the verdant one," the color green symbolizing illumination.

Sufi teaching reached a peak in Europe in the mystery schools of Moorish Spain with the works of Ibn Arabi, and then slowly began to permeate into Christian Europe along with a Christianized version of the Kabbala—a process that gathered momentum through the Sufi links with the Knights Templar. Like the Sufis before them, the Templars were initiates on a path to spiritual enlightenment who used their insights for the benefit of the society in which they moved. Thus by the end of the twelfth century a wide variety of Gnostic and heretical streams had coalesced in secret and exerted a subtle, yet profound, formative influence over cultural developments in Western Europe. Sufi input, Jewish Kabbalistic thoughts and their Christian derivatives were added to Hebraic Gnosticism, a combination which built upon the Rex Deus foundations that had long been established as an underground stream in Christian thinking.

THE MEDIEVAL CRAFTMASONS OF FRANCE

Initiatory orders had long existed among the craftsmen who built the churches, cathedrals, and castles of Europe in Italy, France, England, and elsewhere. Known in England as the

Craftmasons, in France there were several distinct Orders: The Children of Father Soubise, the Children of Master Jacques, and the Children of Solomon whose heirs are known today as Les Compagnons des Devoirs du Tour de France, or the Compagnonnage. All these brotherhoods had some beliefs in common: they observed a moral tradition of chivalry within their craft, a profound humility toward the work that must be done, and above all, they were men who knew how to use a pair of compasses, and who all shared the same bread. Men who know how to use a pair of compasses have been initiated into the secret knowledge of "sacred geometry," qualifying them as "masons." Their perception of the divine origins of their skills was delineated by the English author Ian Dunlop when he wrote: "It is not uncommon in medieval illumination to find God the Father represented as the '*elegans architectus*' holding a large pair of compasses."

Initiated masons formed a hierarchy of three ascending degrees: apprentice, companion, and master mason. Apprentices learned their trade moving from yard to yard throughout the country in what was described as a *Tour de France*, receiving instruction from highly skilled and initiated men known as companions. When the required degree of skill had been attained, they in turn were initiated by their masters in secret conclaves known as cayennes. The three principal fraternities that centuries later merged into one had different duties, skills, and their own distinctive traditions. The Children of Father Soubise built in the Romanesque style and could be found at the very heart of the Benedictine monastic system. Their mason's marks, or "signatures," differ greatly from those of their brethren who built in the Gothic style. The traditions of the *Compagnons Passants du Devoir*, or the Children of Master Jacques, claim that Master Jacques was the son of Jacquin who had been made a master Craftmason after an apprenticeship served in Greece, Egypt, and Jerusalem. Indeed, it is alleged that Jacquin made the two pillars of the Temple of Solomon.

THE CHILDREN OF SOLOMON AND THE TEMPLARS

The third fraternity, the Children of Solomon, is perhaps the most important of our investigations into the origins of

BENEDICTINE CHURCH AND ABBEY IN TUSCANY BUILT IN THE OLD ROMANESQUE STYLE, WITH ITS ROUND-ARCHED WINDOWS AND DOORS, AND MASSIVE STONE WALLS.

Freemasonry. They built Chartres Cathedral and most of the other great Gothic cathedrals, such as Rheims and Amiens, which are all marked with their signature, the *chrisme à l'epée*, a Celtic cross enclosed in a circle. They were taught the principles of sacred geometry by Cistercian monks. Significantly, they were named after King Solomon who was responsible for the building of the first Temple in Jerusalem. Another branch of the Compagnonnage who built many of the Templar churches in the south of France was known as the Compagnonnage Tuscana, and its traditions trace the origins of its mysteries back to Egypt and Biblical Israel via Roman and Greek routes. They claimed to be part of the ancient *collegia* of constructors known as *les Tignarii* that had been founded by the Roman initiate Numa Pompilius.

The precise nature of the relationship between the Children of Solomon and the Templars is mysterious. It is far from clear whether this Order of Craftmasons was an integral part of the knightly Order, affiliated with it in an undocumented manner, or just associated with it by usage. What is known is that, at the behest of Bernard of Clairvaux, the Knights Templar gave a rule to this fraternity in March 1145 that was prefaced by the words:

> *We the Knights of Christ and of the Temple follow the destiny that prepares us to die for Christ. We have the wish to give this rule of living, of work, and of honor to the constructors of churche that Christianity can spread throughout the Earth not so that our name should be remembered, O Lord, but that Your Name should live.*

An indication that the Children of Solomon were indeed affiliated in some way with the Order of the Templars lies in the fact that they were granted great privileges by the Church and government of that time, which included freedom from all taxes, like the Templars, and they were also protected against any form of prosecution by the constructors of other buildings. When the Templars were suppressed in 1314, the Children of Solomon were immediately stripped of these privileges and immunities.

The Knights Templar, through their financial activities, were intimately involved in the era of cathedral construction known as the Rise of the Gothic as the English architectural historian Fred Gettings makes clear:

> *The Knights Templar who were founded ostensibly to protect the pilgrimage routes to the Holy Land, were almost openly involved in financing and lending moral support to the building of Cathedrals throughout Europe.*

Both the twentieth-century initiate, Fulcanelli, and the author Kenneth Rayner Johnson claim that Gothic architecture, which was the fruit of the Templar's knowledge of sacred geometry, was not merely an example of architectural beauty but also a three-dimensional code that passed a hidden message in an architectural form of *la langue verte*, the language of initiation. They were confirming the view expressed in different words nearly a century earlier by J. F. Colfs, who wrote: "The language of stones spoken by this new art [Gothic architecture] is at the same time clear and sublime, speaking alike to the humblest and to the most cultured heart."

La langue verte arises from the need for heretical initiates to hide the true nature of their conversations from the Church hierarchy. In this way, heretics could communicate in code without putting either their lives or their freedom in jeopardy. This clever form of defense against persecution became the language not only of the initiates but also of all the poor and oppressed, and was the true medieval ancestor of cockney rhyming slang and the verbiage in American hip-hop slang and rap.

GOTHIC ARCHITECTURE

STYLE OF FORMAL BUILDING IN EUROPE BETWEEN THE TWELFTH AND THE SIXTEENTH CENTURIES, CHARACTERIZED BY INTERIOR HEIGHT FEATURING PILLARS, ARCHES, AND RIB VAULTING, AND EXTERIOR SOLIDITY FEATURING WALLS SUPPORTED BY FLYING BUTTRESSES; IN ENGLAND, GOTHIC ARCHITECTURE BEGINS AS "EARLY ENGLISH," MOVES THROUGH "DECORATED," AND ENDS AS "PERPENDICULAR."

CHARTRES CATHEDRAL, A GLORIOUS EXAMPLE OF THE NEW GOTHIC STYLE OF ARCHITECTURE WITH WHICH THE CRAFTMASONS LITERALLY REACHED NEW HEIGHTS OF BUILDING.

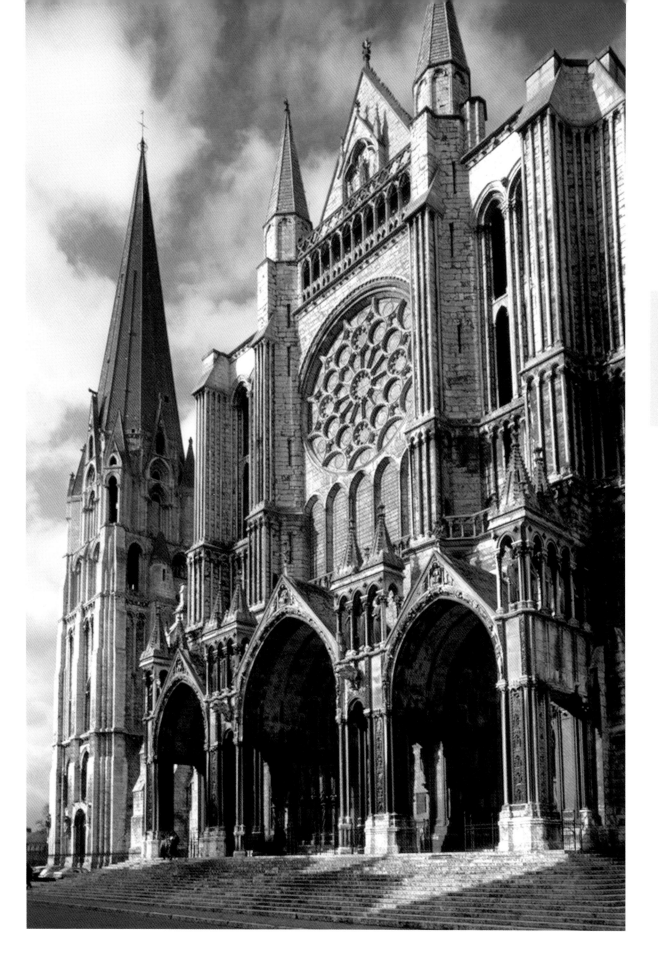

SACRED GEOMETRY

Sacred geometry is a divinely inspired art form that was handed down from master to novice in an unbroken chain from the earliest times until the fall of Jerusalem in 70 CE. This initiatory chain of communication transmitted the secret knowledge used by the Ancient Egyptians and Biblical Israelites to construct their sacred buildings. Knowledge of sacred geometry was apparently lost after the destruction of the temple until the Knights Templar returned to Europe from Jerusalem in 1128, after completing their excavations under the Temple Mount. Indeed, there is a definite cause-and-effect relationship between the Templars' return from Jerusalem and the sudden explosion of building in the Gothic style that followed. Did the Templars find the keys to this new form of building under the Temple Mount? Or were other influences at play in Jerusalem that can explain this new form of architecture? There is absolutely no discernible transition in Europe between Romanesque architecture and the new, tall, graceful form of the Gothic cathedrals. The Gothic style was indeed a startlingly new and beautiful development—but what were its origins?

GOTHIC ARCHITECTURE

In earlier works we have suggested one possible source for Gothic architecture—namely documentation discovered under the Temple Mount—but architectural development at the time of the Temple would not have included arches of any kind. Both Egyptian and Hebraic architecture were both based on transverse lintels, not arches. In fact, the only influence that might have stimulated the creation of an arch at that time was Roman.

Gordon Strachan, a long-time associate of Keith Critchlow who has devoted most of his life to an in-depth study of sacred architecture, has come up with a theory that has the merit of simplicity and credibility—one that is totally consistent with the known level of cultural interchange that took place in the Holy Land both during the First Crusade and thereafter. Strachan echoes other authors such as William Anderson when he suggests that the pointed arch that is the foundation of the Gothic style of building came from the Holy Land. He describes it as "a unique blending of

European building skills with the architectural genius of Islam." The Templars during their first nine years in Jerusalem met many Sufis who, like their Rex Deus counterparts in Europe, followed an initiatory spiritual pathway. According to Strachan, the Templars learned the manner of designing the Islamic *mukhammas* pointed arch from the Sufis and used it to build a three-bayed doorway with pointed arches on the Temple Mount: arches that can still be seen today. Thus, knowledge of sacred geometry gained an immense boost from contact between the initiatory Orders of both faiths, the Templars and the Sufis. Gordon Strachan would seem to be correct, for the fruits of this inter-faith architectural legacy can still be seen and appreciated in the medieval Gothic cathedrals that were largely financed by the Knights Templar and built by the Children of Solomon.

Ouspensky noted the importance of Templar influence on these buildings in the last century when he wrote:

The building of cathedrals was part of a colossal and cleverly devised plan which permitted the existence of entirely free philosophical and psychological schools in

A PORTION OF THE FRIEZE ABOVE THE TRIPLE DOORWAY OF THE WEST FRONT OF CHARTRES, SHOWING JESUS' TRIUMPHAL ENTRY INTO JERUSALEM AND ENTOMBMENT, BUT DELIBERATELY OMITTING THE CRUCIFIXION.

the rude, absurd, cruel, superstitious, bigoted and scholastic Middle Ages. These schools have left us an immense heritage, almost all of which we have already wasted without understanding its meaning and value.

Fulcanelli, in his work *Le Mystère des Cathédrales*, stated that a church or cathedral was not merely a place of worship, or a sanctuary for the sick and deprived, but also a place of commercial activity, public theater, and secular beliefs.

The Gothic cathedral, that sanctuary of the Tradition, Science and Art, should not be regarded as a work dedicated solely to the glory of Christianity, but rather as a vast concretion of ideas, of tendencies, of popular beliefs; a perfect whole to which we can refer without fear, whenever we would penetrate the religious secular, philosophic or social thoughts of our ancestors.

Indeed, according to Fulcanelli, these Gothic cathedrals acted like a philosophical "stock exchange" in which lingering pockets of arcana and heresy were flaunted under the noses of the unsuspecting clergy.

CHARTRES CATHEDRAL

Chartres cathedral is the supreme example of sacred architecture in the Christian world portraying the truths that lead humanity closer to God. It is a hymn to Gnostic initiatory spirituality; a melodic symphony in stone that visibly celebrates divine harmony. Every pilgrim or tourist, regardless of his or her faith or lack of it, leaves the building spiritually uplifted, inspired, and transformed. That is the true measure of the enduring magic of this cathedral. Chartres has long been known as the Golden Book in which inspired sages have inscribed their wisdom as a lasting legacy to all who seek spiritual truth.

The west front of Chartres Cathedral contains the three main doors and, in a frieze that runs just above the lintels of these doors, there are 38 scenes from the life of Jesus carved in detail. Significantly, these do not include a carving of the Crucifixion—indeed, nowhere in the cathedral is there a carving of the Crucifixion that dates from the twelfth century. This startling omission of any commemoration of the central tenet of Christian dogma is quite deliberate. It is a reflection of the Templar belief that Jesus came to reveal and not to redeem.

There are three initiatory Black Madonnas in Chartres. The first is a modern replica of a medieval copy of the Druidic statue of the Virgini Pariturae, described by Caesar. It can be found in the crypt, which, as the official guide categorically states, was used as an initiation chamber. Another can be found in the Ambulatory of the main cathedral and is known as the Virgin of the Pillar. The Virgin is clothed, according to tradition, in heavy, ornate robes shaped formally in a triangle. She stands on a place of tangible energy, a place of God-given power where the vibration is especially low and which is said to induce a feeling of faintness, indicating that this is a point of spiritual transformation. The third initiatory Black Madonna is carved in neither wood nor stone but is instead depicted in stained glass. *Notre Dame de la Belle Verrière*, as it is known, miraculously survived not only the fire that destroyed the earlier Romanesque cathedral but also centuries of strife, including the French Revolution and two World Wars. Within the cathedral are many other points of telluric power that have the capacity to raise one to a point of etheric enhancement, to a true "state of grace," a quality that was recognized, used, and enhanced by the craftsmen who created this magnificent building.

ONE OF THE MANY ALCHEMICAL QUATREFOILS
ON THE WEST FRONT OF AMIENS
CATHEDRAL DEPICTING SPIRITUAL
TRANSFORMATION IN THE ALLEGORICAL
FORM OF THE TRANSMUTATION OF
BASE METAL INTO GOLD.

AMIENS CATHEDRAL

The west front of Amiens Cathedral, the largest cathedral in France, is profusely decorated with quatrefoils depicting alchemical symbolism representing not the transmutation of base metals into gold but the spiritual transformation of base humanity into the gold of spiritual enlightenment. Alchemy is merely an allegory for initiation.

The French mystical writer François Cali describes traveling from Chartres to Amiens as a journey in which one makes an almost imperceptible transition "from the love of God to the love of wisdom, which can be found in Order, number, and harmony, and is equated with God." Order, number, and harmony are all attributes of the divine Gnosis so treasured by the Templar knights and in this cathedral are used to create a wondrous, symphonic blend of space, stone, and light, deliberately designed to celebrate the Gnostic principle of sophia or sacred wisdom. Amiens Cathedral, the rebuilding of which after a fire was financed by the Templars, was used to house the Knights Templars' most precious relic: the reliquary containing the severed head of John the Baptist. According to the late Guy Jordan—noted Provençal scholar of Templarism—this object of veneration is nothing less than *la vrai tête Baphometique Templier*, the true Baphometic head of the Templars.

There are carved panels in the transept depicting the story of John the Baptist, all colored in the medieval fashion and, furthermore, the outer wall of the choir is decorated with superb bas-reliefs that depict his life and death, including one where the top of his severed head is being pierced by a knife. The significance of this piercing is unclear, but its importance to the Templars can be seen—in their burial practices. A Templar church in Bargemon in the Var has had part of its floor replaced with a transparent perspex sheet, allowing a clear view of the human remains in the crypt beneath. A row of skulls and long bones can be seen and each skull is pierced in the manner depicted at Amiens.

The importance of John the Baptist to the Templars is reinforced by a passage from the Gospel of Thomas in which Jesus is quoted as saying:

Among those born of women, from Adam until John the Baptist, there is no one so superior to John the Baptist that his eyes should not be lowered (before him).

Churches dedicated to St. John the Baptist are numerous throughout the Languedoc and Provence, lands once subject to Templar rule. In one, at Trigance near the Gorges de Verdon, an ingenious arrangement allows a beam of light to illuminate the altar with a golden glow at dawn on the Baptist's feast day. Nearby is a Templar chateau built to protect the area against incursions by the Saracens. In many of these Provençal churches and chapels there are numerous carvings of John the Baptist, yet contemporary carvings of the Crucifixion are notable by their absence. Furthermore, in many cases these churches are noted not only for their alchemical symbolism, but also for being homes to the Black Madonna.

COLORED CARVING OF SALOME INCISING
THE SEVERED HEAD OF ST. JOHN THE
BAPTIST TO BE FOUND IN THE SOUTH
TRANSEPT OF AMIENS CATHEDRAL.

the holy grail and the templars

THE KNIGHTS TEMPLAR (KNOWN FOR CENTURIES AS "THE KNIGHTS OF THE HOLY GRAIL"), AND THE AUTHOR OF THE FIRST GRAIL SAGA, ORIGINATE FROM ONE OF THE LEADING REX DEUS FAMILIES.

M any people throughout Europe and the Christian world have been familiar with Rex Deus legends and stories for centuries yet are, at the same time, completely oblivious to their heretical origins and true import. The stroke of genius that led to the composition and dissemination of the stories of the search for the Holy Grail truly immortalized the spiritual teaching of Rex Deus. This literary genre was created simply to spread the initiatory teachings of Jesus far beyond the narrow confines of the families who were descended from the high priests of the Temple in Jerusalem and outward into the consciousness of the general public.

The Grail sagas are a clever amalgam of pre-Christian traditions with a Christian gloss and containing a coded guide to the true teachings of Jesus. The Grail itself is described as a chalice, a cup, a stone that fell from heaven, a stone within a cup, or a magical bowl, and is believed to be capable of restoring life to the dead or good health to the wounded or infirm. It is represented as the "stone within the cup" carried by Melchizedek in the carving of this priest-king of Jerusalem that stands in the Portal of the Initiates by the north door of Chartres Cathedral, or as the cup of Joseph of Arimathea carried by a monk depicted at Rosslyn Chapel.

THE ORIGIN OF THE GRAIL SAGAS

Tracing the origin of the twelfth-century Grail sagas brings us back again to the Rex Deus families in the city of Troyes in the twelfth century. The first Grail romance was circulated as an unfinished epic, *Perceval*, or *Le Conte del Graal*, written by Chrétien de Troyes around 1190. Chrétien was a priest who became a noted translator and a writer of considerable repute and was yet another relative of Hughes de Payen. His three earlier works were dedicated to Marie, Countess of Champagne, who was the daughter of King Louis VII of France and Eleanor of Aquitaine. He intended also to dedicate *Le Conte del Graal* to her but Marie retired from public life when her husband, Count Henry, died shortly after his return from the Holy Land. Chrétien was

CARVINGS IN THE PORTAL OF THE INITIATES, CHARTRES CATHEDRAL. MELCHIZEDEK IS SHOWN CARRYING

THE GRAIL, OR CHALICE. NEXT TO MELCHIZADEK ARE ABRAHAM (LEFT) AND MOSES.

A LEADING REX DEUS FAMILY

THE COUNTS OF CHAMPAGNE WERE ONE OF THE MOST IMPORTANT FAMILIES OF THE REX DEUS GROUP IN EUROPE. THEY PLAYED A LEADING ROLE IN THE FOUNDATION OF THE KNIGHTS TEMPLAR, AND WERE THE ORIGINAL PATRONS OF CHRETIEN DE TROYES, THE AUTHOR OF THE FIRST GRAIL SAGA.

forced to seek a new patron and chose another leading member of Rex Deus, Philippe d'Alsace, the Count of Flanders, son of Payen de Montdidier (one of the first nine members of the Knights Templar, and a close relative of the early Christian kings of Jerusalem).

Europe was, in effect, a police state at that time: anyone perceived as being spiritually or religiously different risked being burned at the stake, and as a result members of Rex Deus had to dissemble simply in Order to survive. And so, whereas the Grail stories appear to describe a long and dangerous quest for the most holy of all religious relics, the communion cup from the Last Supper that was later used to collect Jesus' blood at Golgotha by Joseph of Arimathea, the story of Perceval clothed a very different message in allegorical form. The romances describe an arduous quest wherein Perceval, the hero, is exposed to many temptations and physical dangers that replicate the perils of prolonged pilgrimage. This immediately struck a chord with all who heard these stories, for this was the age of deep veneration of holy relics and the sagas were, at first hearing at least, acceptable to the hierarchy of the time. This acceptance was short-lived, however, for they were soon clearly perceived to be an allegorical guide to an alchemical quest; a heretical guide to a pathway to spiritual enlightenment.

THE GRAIL QUEST

Chrétien was soon followed by another writer, Wolfram von Essenbach, who some authorities claim was actually a Templar. Their Grail sagas contain clues to the Rex Deus belief system that flatly contradicted the creed of the oppressive medieval Church. The king of the Grail castle, the Fisher King, is to some degree an allegory for the Church at that time. Being wounded, he imperfectly serves his impoverished realm in a manner similar to the Church, which, having distorted the true teachings of Jesus, despoils the lives of those it claims to serve. In the Grail sagas, the Fisher King's wasted kingdom will only be restored when someone pure enough to see the Grail restores him to full health. Thus the allegory suggests that when the true teachings of Jesus triumph over dogma, corruption, and distortion, heaven will truly be made manifest upon Earth.

The late Trevor Ravenscroft, in *The Cup of Destiny*, shows that the Grail romances reveal, within their drama and symbolism, signposts to a unique path of initiation: namely the true teaching of Jesus.

The world's leading authority on mythology, the late Professor Joseph Campbell, agreed. He declared that the full import of the Grail sagas can be found within a passage from the Gospel of Thomas, where Jesus is reported as saying, "He who drinks from my mouth will become as I am, and I shall be he." To Campbell this is the ultimate form of enlightenment, the true Holy Grail. So the Grail Quest is far from what it seems; there is a hidden agenda here, deliberately and cleverly designed to conceal a vibrant heretical truth from the prying eyes of the clergy. The original Grail sagas are simply coded guides to initiation.

We need to ask ourselves why, in the medieval era, should any knight, however devout, seek the Holy Grail when his personal salvation was guaranteed if he volunteered for duty in the Holy Land—for, according to Papal decree, this service guaranteed absolution for all sins, both those already committed and any that might be committed in the future. Knights Templar or other Crusaders killed in battle went straight to heaven—so why should they seek the Grail? Indeed, what was so holy or special about the Grail? Relics pertaining to Jesus may have been rare, but they

A CLASSICAL DEPICTION OF TEMPLARS FIGHTING SARACENS ON THE RAMPARTS OF THE CITY OF ACRE.

A LATE-MEDIEVAL DEPICTION
OF SIR GALAHAD, SIR
PERCEVAL, AND SIR BORS
CARRYING A SILVER CASE
CONTAINING THE HOLY GRAIL
TO SARRAS IN FRANCE.

did exist and were accessible. Furthermore, the miracle of transubstantiation ensured that simply by attending mass and taking communion in any church or cathedral, a knight would be granted immediate access to the actual body and blood of Jesus.

THE IMPORTANCE OF MYTH AND LEGEND

Myth and legend have been employed for millennia to carry spiritual allegories and politically uncomfortable truths into the public consciousness. At the beginning of the twentieth century, scholars tended to dismiss these myths as "inspired fiction" and steadfastly ignored the fact that tribal, national, and religious traditions, including Christianity, deliberately generate their own mythologies to buttress their belief systems. Thanks to Joseph Campbell and others like him, there has been a radical revision of the true value of mythology. Myths are now known to be understood at many levels and are often a useful signpost to truth. Joseph Campbell himself declared that: "Mythology is the penultimate truth, because the ultimate cannot be put into words." Ananda Coomeraswamy claims that: "Myth embodies the nearest approach to absolute truth that can be stated in words." Kathleen Raine, the poet, said, "Fact is not the truth

of myth; myth is the truth of fact."

The term "Holy Grail" is often claimed to be a corruption of the term "Holy Gradual," in which the word "gradual" is used in the sense of a slow spiritual ascent or initiatory pathway. In the early 1980s the words "Holy Grail," or *Sangraal* as it is written in French, were defined as a corrupt version of *Sang Real*, or "Holy Blood," in the book *The Holy Blood and the Holy Grail*. This was the first English-language mass publication that stated categorically that Jesus had married and founded a dynasty. It received a very mixed reception, being greeted with howls of protest alleging "blasphemy" and "heresy" on the one hand, and on the other, equally loud cries of "brilliant" and "provocative." This was nothing new, for the original Grail stories also provoked a mixed response—soon after their first publication, they were clearly regarded as a distinct irritant by the Catholic Church. But because by that time they had already gained wide public acceptance, suppression was out of the question. So the Church fell back on a tried and tested formula: it put out its own version and circulated it widely. It created a highly sanitized and censored variation of these stories that was in total conformity with Church doctrine. This "official" version became known as the Vulgate Cycle and later became the foundation for later writers such as Thomas Mallory, whose *Morte d'Arthur* in 1469 sealed the link between the Arthurian legends and the Grail sagas. The Church had apparently solved the problem of the heresy in the original sagas, in a manner that was to endure for centuries.

THE INHERENT HERESY OF THE GRAIL

Heresy within the original sagas was obvious to any educated reader, for the hidden code within the stories was not particularly subtle. For example, Wolfram von Essenbach said of himself that he could neither read nor write:

I do not know a single letter of the alphabet. Plenty of people get their material that way, but this adventurer steers without books. Rather than have anyone think this is a book, I would sit naked without a towel, the way I would sit in the bath—if I didn't forget the fig leaf!

Trevor Ravenscroft said of this passage:

The clue to the question of the so-called illiteracy of Wolfram von Essenbach is in his sly sense of humor within the last sentence of this enigmatic passage. ... The fig leaf has always been the symbol of the occult initiate who has developed supersensible faculties and entered into higher realms of consciousness.

This admission of illiteracy was an oblique way of claiming that Wolfram could see into the spiritual world and read the occult script, and, significantly, he also claimed that the source for his inspiration was an individual named as Kyot of Provence whom he had met in Toledo, Spain. In the early thirteenth century Toledo was a city wherein students of the Sufi tradition mixed freely with Jewish Kabbalistic scholars and Rex Deus adherents of the true teachings of Jesus. Indeed, as I have mentioned above, it is within Sufism that we find the earliest record of the transmission of spiritual knowledge from master to Initiate.

THE HERESY OF THE BLACK MADONNA

It is no coincidence that the peak years of the development of the cult of the Black Madonna fall well within the Templar era and that most of the effigies are located in areas of that Order's influence. Yet, while Mariolatry is of incalculable importance to the Catholic Church, it has always been uncomfortable with the cult of the Black Madonna. One clue to this may be found in the words of Bernard of Clairvaux.

At the time of the Council of Troyes, Bernard laid down a specific requirement for all the members of the Templars to make "obedience to Bethany and the House of Mary and Martha"—in other words, to swear obedience and loyalty to the dynasty founded by Mary Magdalene and Jesus. Indeed, many scholars now believe that the great Notre Dame cathedrals built or financed by the Templars were dedicated not to Mary the mother of Jesus, but to Mary Magdalene and the son of Jesus.

The Templar veneration of the Magdalene in the guise of the Black Madonna was widespread, and the author, Ean Begg, lists over 50 centers of veneration of the Black Madonna in churches dedicated to the Magdalene. According to the beliefs of the hidden stream of spirituality within Christianity, the Magdalene is "the symbol of divine wisdom" and according to the Nazorean tradition, she was depicted garbed in black like the priestess Isis, surmounted by Sophia's crown of stars, and her infant wore the golden crown of royalty. Ean Begg claimed many years before the disclosure of the Rex Deus tradition that the history and legends of the Black Virgin reveal a heretical sect with the power to shock and astonish even current post-Christian attitudes, one that involves political forces still influential in Europe today—a comment that, in the light of Rex Deus revelations, is right on the mark!

The majority of the Knights Templar—many of the knights, all the serjeants, craftsmen, and auxiliary members —were undoubtedly staunch followers of the Catholic faith, but the founders and the real leaders thereafter were the "heretics" and Gnostics. The French scholars Georges Caggar and Jean Robin claim that:

The Order of the Temple was indeed constituted of seven exterior circles dedicated to the minor mysteries, and of three interior circles corresponding to the initiation into the great mysteries. The nucleus was composed of 70 Templars ...

AN EARLY ENGRAVING OF THE KNIGHTS TEMPLAR. THEY ARE PICTURED HERE VENERATING THE TRUE CROSS, BEFORE ENTERING BATTLE AGAINST THE SARACENS IN THE HOLY LAND.

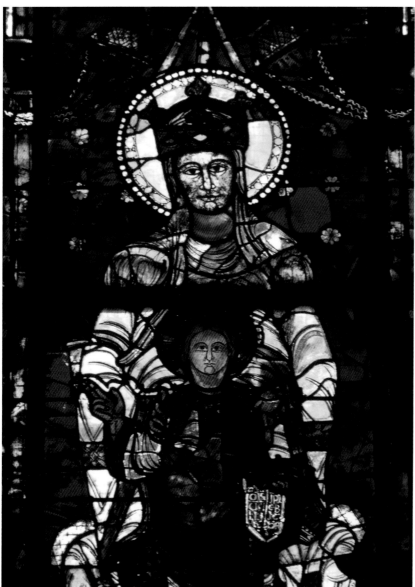

LA DAME DE LA BELLE VERRIERE,
AN 11TH CENTURY STAINED GLASS
WINDOW AT CHARTRES, ONE OF THE
THREE INITIATORY BLACK VIRGINS
WITHIN THE CATHEDRAL.

of acute financial difficulties. To ease his plight, Philippe first levied a 10-per-cent tax on the Church and imposed punitive financial measures on the Languedoc. Forced loans were frequently imposed throughout the country and the King repeatedly debased the coinage. This provoked riot and civil commotion and the king sought refuge in the Paris temple, the headquarters of the Knights Templar. Later, the Lombard bankers to whom he owed over 800,000 *livres tournois* were despoiled and their assets seized. The Jews were another obvious target, and, in 1295 their "usurious profits" were confiscated, and in July and August of 1306 all Jewish property throughout France was seized and the penniless dispossessed owners expelled from the country.

Membership of the secretive ruling clique was restricted to known members of Rex Deus. Yet despite their power, all we have left to trace their beliefs are the Grail sagas, the cult of the Black Madonna, and traces that eventually carried over into later Freemasonry, for this seemingly all-powerful Order was to endure a brutal and remarkably rapid fall from grace due to the greed and cupidity of a French King.

KING PHILIPPE LE BEL

King Philippe IV succeeded to the throne of France in October 1285 at a time when the kingdom was in the grip

FRIDAY 13TH

As dawn broke on Friday October 13, 1307, the king's agents throughout France opened sealed Orders that had been distributed a month earlier. Then, French soldiers raided every Templar property within the kingdom, arresting the Templar Grand Master, and the 60 knights of the inner circle. Only 24 of the senior members of the

Order residing in France, including Gerard de Villiers, the preceptor of France, managed to escape.

Charges were leveled against the Templars that were described as: "A bitter thing, a lamentable thing, a thing which is horrible to contemplate, terrible to hear of, a detestable crime, an execrable evil, an abominable work, a detestable disgrace, a thing almost inhuman, indeed set apart from all humanity." The Order stood accused of heresy —not because of its true beliefs, which stayed secret, but because of Philippe le Bel's need for money.

The king explained that he was acting at the request of the chief inquisitor of France, but it is obvious that Philippe was the prime mover in the whole affair, and that in this instance, the inquisition was acting as an arm of the state and not at the behest of the pope (who was not informed of the arrests until after the event). The knights were tortured for many years, and of the 138 depositions from the interrogations in Paris that October—which included those of Jacques de Molay and his leading knights—only four testify that the men concerned were able to withstand the horrors to which they were subjected. Pope Clement V lacked both the power and the will to halt the proceedings, but on November 22, 1307 he ordered the Christian rulers in Europe to arrest all Templars and confiscate their properties in his own name.

The English king, who had previously refused to give "easy credence" to the charges against the Templars, now had no choice in the matter and replied that he would initiate action against the knights in "the quickest and best way." Few knights were actually arrested and imprisoned; most were allowed to stay in their preceptories and, because torture was forbidden under English law, no one confessed to heresy when interrogated. Proceedings in England were unproductive until after June 1311, when papal pressure resulted in the use of torture. As a result, one knight—a certain Stephen de Stapelbrugge—confessed to denying Christ and claimed that homosexuality had been encouraged within the Order. In Portugal the Order was put on trial and the verdict was "not guilty"; in Scotland the trial of the Templars brought in the Scottish verdict

KING PHILIP IV OF FRANCE (1268–1314), PHILIP LE BEL, WHO ORDERED THE ARREST OF THE TEMPLARS.

of "not proven." The archbishop of Compostela in Spain pleaded with the pope, begging that the Templars be acquitted, because their skills and resources were desperately needed in the wars against the Moorish forces in Spain. The Rex Deus family of the House of Savoy, who ruled Lombardy, ensured that the bishops in their realm supported the Templar cause, and those bishops issued a statement claiming that they could find no incriminating evidence against the Order. In other lands the results were less favorable and convictions were achieved; in Germany and in Greece the results were mixed. In France, however, the agony of the Templars continued until it reached its fiery finale in 1314, when the Templar Grand Master Jacques de Molay and Geoffroi de Charney were sentenced to a lingering death on the Isle des Javiaux, where a slow, hot, and smokeless fire was prepared to ensure that the Templars' agony would be as prolonged as possible. Both Jacques de Molay and Geoffroi de Charnay were slowly

cooked to death. As he died, Jacques de Molay cursed Pope Clement V and King Philippe le Bel, and called upon them both to appear before God in heaven within the year—and strange to relate, both the accursed king and the pope heeded that prophetic call.

PAPAL SUPPRESSION OF THE ORDER

Whatever the truth or falsehood of the charges against individuals may have been, the actual Order of the Knights Templars was never convicted of any of them. Nonetheless a decision to suppress the Order was announced in the papal bull *Vox in excelso* issued on March 22, 1312. The reasons for the suppression were as follows:

> *considering, moreover, the grave scandal which has arisen from these things against the Order, which it did not seem could be checked while this Order remained in being . . . even without blame being attached to the brothers . . . not by judicial sentence, but by way of provision, or apostolic ordinance, we abolish the aforesaid Order of the Temple . . . and we subject it to perpetual prohibition . . . Which if anyone acts against this, he will incur the sentence of excommunication ipso facto.*

The Order's vast estates, financial assets, and other possessions were mostly transferred to the rival Order of the Knights Hospitallers, with some exceptions made in the kingdoms of Castile, Aragon, Portugal, and Majorca. In France deductions were authorized in favor of King Philippe to cover the imprisonment and interrogation of the knights of the Order; and in this way the Templars were made to pay for their own incarceration and torture.

The fate of the treasure that the king of France saw during his stay in the Paris temple, and of the considerable sums he had observed being carried into the temple when Jacques de Molay and his large train arrived from La Rochelle shortly before the arrests, is a mystery that still provokes intense speculation. When the king's seneschals raided the temple, the treasure had vanished, and by the time his troops reached La Rochelle, the Templar's Atlantic fleet, along with the 18 ships that had carried Jacques de Molay and his retinue from Cyprus, had disappeared, destination unknown!

According to a long-standing legend that is apparently confirmed by much later French Free-Masonic tradition, the destination of most of the vanished treasure was the land of Scotland, to which we must now turn to study the first clear signs of the transformative process that changed the medieval Craftmasons' guilds into Speculative Freemasonry.

FULFILLMENT OF THE CURSE

LEGEND RECOUNTS THAT AT THE EXECUTION OF THE LAST KING OF FRANCE, DURING THE FRENCH REVOLUTION, A MAN LEAPT ON TO THE SCAFFOLD, DIPPED HIS HANDS IN THE KING'S BLOOD, HELD THEM ALOFT, AND CRIED: "JACQUES DE MOLAY, THOU ART AVENGED!"

LEFT: THE BURNING OF JACQUES DE MOLAY, THE GRAND MASTER OF THE TEMPLARS, ON THE ILE DES JAVIAUX.

ABOVE: JACQUES DE MOLAY (1244–1314), THE LAST GRAND MASTER OF THE ORDER OF KNIGHTS TEMPLAR.

scottish beginnings

THE MOST LIKELY ACCOUNT OF THE TRANSFORMATION OF THE MEDIEVAL
CRAFTMASONS INTO MODERN FREEMASONRY PLACES THIS IMPORTANT EVENT
IN THE VICINITY OF ROSLIN, NEAR EDINBURGH, SCOTLAND.

The suppression of the Templars created a hiatus in the activities of Rex Deus but it did not end them, for the families had a sacred duty to preserve the spiritual traditions of the Templars and continued to pass on their sacred knowledge in a manner that led eventually to the creation of Freemasonry, Rosicrucianism, the "Invisible College," and the Royal Society in England. They exerted an enormous influence on the people who brought about the Italian Renaissance and, as a result, helped to transform the thinking, art, commerce, social, and religious systems of the entire European continent. In so doing they made a significant contribution to the creation of a culture in which science, democracy, and intellectual freedom could flourish.

> *Nearly all the major intellectual figures of the period— including many of the founding fathers of modern science down to Newton's day—were deeply invested in .... esoteric traditions, as if they believed there might lay hidden in these buried sources secrets of human nature and the universe that were nowhere else to be found.*
> Theodore Roszak, *The Unfinished Animal*

The Catholic Church continued to try to limit and control all access to knowledge. Rex Deus, the Templars, and medieval Craftmasons, on the other hand, believed that *Ars sina scienta nihil est*—Art without knowledge is nothing.

For once in our investigation of the origins of Freemasonry, archaeology, historical records, and local tradition combine to grant us a degree of certainty as to where to look for the coalescing of the hidden streams of spirituality and their first surfacing in a form that is recognizably a precursor to Freemasonry—and that place of transformation is Roslin, in Scotland.

THE LORDLY LINE OF THE HIGH ST. CLAIRS

Following the demise of the Templars and the disappearance of their treasure, the fortunes of one leading Scottish Templar family, the St. Clairs of Roslin, underwent a dramatic improvement. The St. Clairs, who were already wealthy, suddenly became what we would now call "super-rich." A later Baron of Roslin who also became the third

St. Clair Earl of Orkney—William St. Clair, who was renowned for his incredible wealth—was the architect and builder of Rosslyn Chapel, a unique library in stone of arcane symbolism, a sacred building that is now revered by many as the core church of Freemasonry. He was initiated into some of the leading chivalric Orders in Europe, being described as a "Knight of the Cockle and Golden Fleece," as "one of the Illuminati," or as "a nobleman with singular talents," and as "a man of exceptional talents much given

FAR LEFT: THE SUPERBLY DECORATIVE PINNACLES AND FLYING BUTTRESSES OF ROSSLYN CHAPEL.

ABOVE: SIR WILLIAM ST. CLAIR OF ROSLIN, HEREDITARY GRAND MASTER OF THE CRAFTMASONS, WHO RESIGNED HIS HEREDITARY PATRONAGE OF THE CRAFT TO BECOME THE FIRST ELECTED GRAND MASTER OF THE GRAND LODGE OF SCOTLAND.

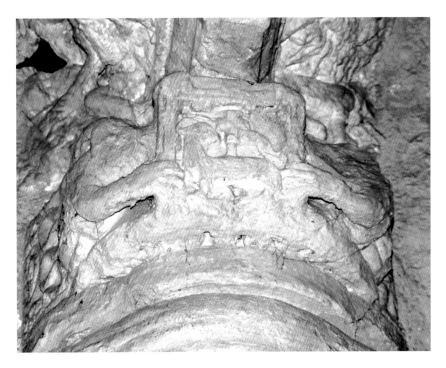

CARVING OF THE TEMPLAR SEAL OF THE AGNUS DEI, FRAMED BY TWO HANDS PARTING A CURTAIN, ROSSLYN CHAPEL.

to policy, such as the buildings of Castles, Palaces and Churches." The Earl was the patron of Craftmasonry throughout Scotland and it is recorded that he was appointed the Grand Master of the Craftmasons and the other hard and soft guilds in Scotland in 1441. It is also interesting to note that, according to Teresa Randford (a director of the Scottish Poetry Library), the name Roslin in Gallic language translates as "ancient knowledge handed down through the generations."

ROSSLYN CHAPEL

Earl William imported skilled and experienced master masons from every part of Europe to build the chapel and considerably enlarged the village of Roslin to accommodate them. For their work on the construction of the chapel, master masons were paid £40 per year, an enormous amount for that time when ordinary masons normally earned £10 per year. The precision that went into the construction of Rosslyn would be described in modern terms as "Quality Assurance," for the Earl exerted sole power of decision over every aspect of the construction, design, and the artwork within it. Designs for the chapel itself, as well as for the carvings, were first drawn out upon "Eastland boards" made from Baltic timber, before being approved by the Earl, and only then were they carved in stone. The result is a symphonic harmony of design that flows naturally from an inspired plan that arose in the mind of a true spiritual giant, one who strode like a Colossus across the divide that separates the late medieval era from the Renaissance. Rosslyn Chapel has exerted mystical appeal to pilgrims of every denomination for over nearly six centuries and has, more recently, been featured in the book and film of *The Da Vinci Code*.

The original plan was to build a great cathedral with a high tower in the center—a form of collegiate church, with "a provost, six prebendaries and two singing boys." The foundations, which were laid in 1446 and were re-excavated at the end of the nineteenth century, confirm that the nave was planned to be 90 feet in length. Small though the present building is, however, what gives the chapel its international reputation is the rich profusion of carvings that have no equal anywhere else. Of the original plan, only the choir is complete, topped by with its strange barrel-vaulted roof built entirely of stone.

EARL WILLIAM ST. CLAIR

EARL WILLIAM ST. CLAIR, EARL OF ORKNEY AND BARON OF ROSLIN, WAS THE ARCHITECT AND BUILDER OF ROSSLYN CHAPEL. HE WAS "A KNIGHT OF THE COCKLE AND GOLDEN FLEECE" WHO WAS ALSO DESCRIBED AS A NOBLEMAN OF "SINGULAR TALENT" AND ONE OF THE "ILLUMINATI."

EARLY INDICATIONS OF FREEMASONRY

The secrecy that shrouds the first three centuries of Freemasonry make it virtually impossible to definitively prove connections between the Freemasons and the other esoteric movements that first came to light at the time of the Renaissance. However, the carvings within Rosslyn chapel indicate of some links with the Rosicrucians as well as displaying a wealth of Masonic symbolism that belies the "official" history of the modern Craft that declares it was only founded in the seventeenth century. For example, the carving of the horned figure of Moses carrying the tablets of the law found in the south aisle is symbolic of one of the Hebraic rites of early Freemasonry, while the weathered carving of the head of Hermes Trimegistos on the exterior of the East wall depicts a common ancestor of many of the European esoteric movements.

THE EXTERIOR

On the outside of the chapel are many flying buttresses, and one is decorated with compasses, symbolic of the Masonic Order. In one of the window bays in the north wall there is a carving of Baphomet, the idol the Templars were accused of worshiping. On the east wall is the head of Hermes Trimegistos and another, more humorous, carving that speaks volumes about the disrespectful way the Craftmasons viewed their clergy, for in it a fox dressed as a clergyman preaches to a flock of geese. In the western window of the south wall is a badly weathered carving of a

Templar knight leading a blindfolded man by a cable-tow noose in the manner of modern Freemasonic Initiation into the First Degree. This is one of very few symbolic representations that link Freemasonic ritual with the Knights Templar.

TEMPLAR SYMBOLISM

The Templar Order had been suppressed for over a century and a half before Rosslyn chapel was founded, yet clearly recognizable Templar symbolism abounds, half-hidden to all except the initiated, in plain sight yet overlooked by all. In the vault of each bay and arching across the vault of the crypt are carvings of the engrailed cross of the Sinclairs with, at the junction of every cross—subtly, but nonetheless distinctly delineated—a form of the distinctive *croix pattée* of the Knights Templar. Not the standard *croix pattée*, but the *croix celeste*, the Gnostic "Cross of Universal Knowledge." Safe in the chapel rests the burial stone of William de Sinncler who, according to family tradition, led the Templar Knights in the final charge that put the invading English to flight at the Battle of Bannockburn, thereby ensuring Scotland's independence. Beside the third window on the north wall at the top of a small pillar is carved a Templar seal in the form of the *agnus dei*. It is no coincidence that the heraldic colors of the St. Clairs of Roslin are argent (silver/white) and sable (black), the same as those of the battle flag of the Templar Order, the beauséante. The St. Clair family motto displayed on the

CARVING OF THE HORNED HEAD OF MOSES IN A WINDOW OF THE SOUTH AISLE, ROSSLYN CHAPEL.

CARVING OF THE HEAD OF HERMES TRIMEGISTOS, EXTERIOR OF EAST WALL, ROSSLYN CHAPEL.

THE CARVING OF THE THREE MAGI ON THE CENTRAL BOSS OF THE RETRO-CHOIR, ROSSLYN CHAPEL.

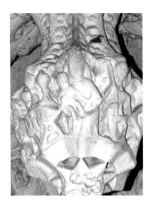

MADONNA AND CHILD ON THE CENTRAL PENDANT BOSS IN THE RETRO-CHOIR, ROSSLYN CHAPEL.

Caithness memorial within the chapel, Commit Thy Verk To God, is remarkably similar to that of the medieval guild known as the Children of Solomon: *Non Nobis Domine. Non Nobis, Sed Nomine Tuo Da Gloriam*, that translates to "Not to us Lord. Not to us, but to your name give all the glory." On one face of the central pendant boss in the retro-choir is a carving of the Madonna and Child and, as we have already seen, veneration of the Black Madonna linked the Templars with other esoteric streams in medieval Europe.

THE ENIGMA OF ROSSLYN CHAPEL

What can we make of carvings in a late medieval Christian church that link to nearly every spiritual influence that obtained in the centuries before Rosslyn was built? So many refer, directly or obliquely, to the initiatory teachings of both the Christian and the pagan eras. Stranger still, a series of carvings commemorate the exploits one of the Earl's distinguished ancestors, Earl Henry St. Clair, the first St. Clair Earl of the Orkneys who made at least two voyages to the New World one hundred years before Columbus. In celebration of his ancestor's epic explorations, Earl William ordered carvings of certain strange plants that had been brought back from America to be placed within the chapel. There are carvings of Aloe cactus, Indian corn or maize, all native American plants which were unknown in Europe at the time of the chapel's construction.

In the south aisle, abreast of the main altar, there is a lintel decorated with scrollwork containing a Latin inscription that translates as "Wine is strong, a King is stronger, women are stronger still, but truth conquers all." From the *Book of Esdras*, this quotes Prince Zerubabel of Judah who used these words to answer a riddle posed in one of King Darius's dreams and was rewarded by being given the king's permission to return to Jerusalem from exile in Babylon and rebuild the Temple. Directly abutting that lintel is an ornately carved pillar around which a legend has grown that is of great significance to modern Freemasonry.

THE "APPRENTICE" PILLAR

Of all the legends that originate in Rosslyn, few are as well known as that surrounding the Apprentice Pillar. The story of

the murdered apprentice with its blatant reference to the much older legend of Hiram Abif, the master mason at the building of King Solomon's Temple in Jerusalem, has immense spiritual and ritual significance not only for the Craftmasons who built this chapel, but for their modern spiritual heirs, the worldwide brotherhood of Freemasonry. The Rosslyn legend recounts that:

The master mason having received from his patron the model of a pillar of exquisite workmanship and design, hesitated to carry it out until he had been to Rome or some such foreign part, and seen the original. He went abroad, and in his absence, an apprentice, having dreamed the finished pillar, at once set to work and carried out the design as it now stands, a perfect marvel of workmanship. The master mason on his return was so stung with envy that he asked who had dared to do it in his absence. On being told it was his own apprentice, he was so inflamed with rage and passion that he struck him with his mallet, killed him on the spot, and paid the penalty for his rash and cruel act.

True or not as the legend may be, the workmanship of the Apprentice Pillar surpasses in skill almost all of the other sculptures in the chapel. The carved head of the "murdered apprentice" can be found tucked away, high in the south-west corner of the clerestory wall, and looks down, not on his own pillar but, surprisingly, on the equally beautiful and serene pillar carved by the master mason himself. Above the Master Mason's Pillar, looking outward into the main body of the chapel, there is a carving of the master mason's head.

Nearby, high on the south clerestory wall, is a weathered carving of the grieving widow, the mother of the apprentice. For millennia, from the time of ancient Egypt down to the present day, the term "The Son of the Widow" has been

LEFT: THE HEAD OF THE "MURDERED APPRENTICE," COMPLETE WITH THE MAUL MARK OF THE TEMPLE, ROSSLYN CHAPEL.

BELOW: THE PILLAR, WHOSE CREATION PROVOKED THE MASTER MASON TO MURDER HIS APPRENTICE OUT OF JEALOUSY.

CARVING OF THE DEATH MASK OF KING
ROBERT THE BRUCE, THE RETRO-CHOIR,
ROSSLYN CHAPEL.

made to attract. Each pillar must be built upon the same rock or foundation, and that rock, in the tradition of Craft Freemasonry, is called truth and justice. This conception of the ideal foundation finds also echoes in the qualities aspired to by any true initiate of Freemasonry:

He who is as wise as a Perfect Master will not be easily injured by his own actions. Hath a person the strength which a Senior Warden represents he will bear and overcome every obstacle in life. He who is adorned like a Junior Warden with humility of spirit approaches nearer to the similitude of God than others.

Gedricke, eighteenth-century Masonic historian

used to describe the true initiates of the spiritual world. In the worldwide fraternity of modern Freemasonry, all are pledged to aid "the son of a widow" who is in distress, for charity and the relief of the suffering of a brother is central to true brotherhood.

THREE PILLARS OF GREAT MASONIC IMPORT

The three pillars that separate the retro-choir from the main chapel are the Apprentice Pillar, the Master Mason's Pillar, and a third, plain fluted pillar between them—the Journeyman's Pillar. The capitals of each of these are decorated with carvings of angels playing medieval instruments. One eighteenth-century Masonic historian claimed that each true lodge should be supported by three grand pillars of deep symbolic significance: one to symbolize "wisdom" (the Mason's Pillar); the second "strength" (the Journeyman's Pillar); and the third, "beauty" (the Apprentice Pillar). Each pillar represents not only the named quality but also its significance and its function, for wisdom constructs, strength supports, and beauty adorns. Also, wisdom is ordained to discover, strength is made to bear, and beauty is

Thus the care that has been lavished upon these three magnificent pillars within Rosslyn Chapel symbolizes the spiritual insight and wisdom that Earl William drew upon to found this mystical shrine.

SPIRITUAL SYMBOLISM

THE CARVINGS WITHIN ROSSLYN CHAPEL ARE RARELY EXPLICITLY AND SOLELY CHRISTIAN. THEY COMMEMORATE IN SYMBOLIC FASHION ALMOST EVERY KNOWN INITIATORY OR GNOSTIC PATHWAY TO ENLIGHTENMENT FROM EARLY HISTORY.

THE RETRO-CHOIR

In the retro-choir or Lady Chapel to the east of the three pillars, there is a large pendant boss hanging from the roof carved to depict the story of the birth of Jesus: on one side is the Madonna and child, on the other the three Magi and the shepherds. On a ribbed arch nearby is possibly the oldest and most complete version of the dance macabre or the "Dance of Death" to be seen anywhere in Europe. All walks of life are represented in this eerie procession, 16 pairs of figures in all, giving vivid illustration to the fact that the only absolute certainty in life is death itself. Tucked away among the carvings of the east wall is a representation of the death mask of King Robert the Bruce, the last Sovereign Commander of the Knights Templar.

THE CRYPT

Steps in the southeast corner of the chapel lead to the crypt. These have been recently refurbished in order to make them safe, for prior to this they were incredibly well-worn, demonstrating that very many pilgrims had visited Rosslyn Chapel in the hundred years or so between its completion and the Reformation. There are working drawings on the north wall of the crypt that have not been precisely dated, but it is known that this area was used as a workshop by the Craftmasons during the construction of the main chapel. Two stones alongside the north wall are imports from outside the chapel, one a Templar gravestone of the thirteenth century, the second a much later, seventeenth-century Guild-stone entitled "The King of Terrors."

Above the steps, in the main chapel, the first window in the south wall is framed by carvings of the maize plants

CARVING OF A BEARDED MAN WITH A GRAIL CHALICE, OFTEN CLAIMED TO BE MELCHIZADEK, THE SOUTH AISLE, ROSSLYN CHAPEL.

ONE OF THE 120 CARVINGS OF THE
GREEN MAN TO BE FOUND WITHIN
ROSSLYN CHAPEL. MEDIEVAL
CARVINGS OF THE GREEN MAN

SYMBOLIZE THE GNOSTIC
PRINCIPLE OF DEATH TO THE
TEMPORAL WORLD AND REBIRTH
IN THE WORLD OF THE SPIRIT.

mentioned previously. On the east side of the next window
is a carving of a bearded, robed man holding a cup or
chalice in both hands—and this is one of the few carvings in
the entire chapel that shows signs of having been subjected
to violence. Look closely at the columnar frame to the right
of this figure: clear marks indicate that this carving has been
struck with some sharp or hard implement. By the south
door there is a small pillar and above its capital are a group
of figures that include St. Veronica holding the veil on which
is depicted the face of Christ. This is a representation of the
"Mandylion" or the "Veil of Veronica," a symbol of great
importance to the Templars. Throughout the chapel, carvings
of the Green Man abound. In the vast confines of Chartres
Cathedral there are only 86, yet here in the small Chapel of
Rosslyn there are over 120 and possibly more. This cross-
cultural symbol of spiritual rebirth was, according to the
English architectural historian William Anderson, a sort of
mascot to the medieval Craftmasons.

THE VICTORIAN STAINED-GLASS WINDOWS

Superb stained-glass windows were installed at Rosslyn in
the later years of the Victorian era, and these clearly
demonstrate that sacred Gnosis still flourished in that era.
There are two windows commemorating Roman soldiers,
one of St. Longinus, the other of St. Mauritius. The figure of
St. Michael the Archangel is displayed in solitary splendor in

STAINED-GLASS WINDOWS AT ROSSLYN

THE FOUR SUPERB STAINED-GLASS WINDOWS IN THE CLERESTORY AT
ROSSLYN CHAPEL WERE SPECIFICALLY COMMISSIONED AND DESIGNED
BY LOCAL FREEMASONS IN LATE-VICTORIAN TIMES.

the window of the south clerestory facing them; he was the
patron saint of the Knights Templar. St. Michael was of
course not only described in the Bible as "the prince of the
Heavenly Hosts," but was also regarded as the Guardian
Angel of ancient Israel. More than that, he was believed to
hold the secret of the "Word" by which God created heaven
and earth—and the parallels here between the "Word" of
creation and the secret Masonic "Word" are self-evident. In
the window immediately opposite St. Michael, between the
windows showing the Roman soldiers, is a figure that, at
first glance, one would hardly expect in a Scottish chapel.
The saint depicted is the patron saint of England, St. George.
Legends surrounding St. George link him closely to St.
Michael and to the Babylonian resurrecting god Tammuz.
Connections between the Sufis and the Templars and
Tammuz may provide further evidence of this. Most
authorities now believe that el Khidir—the mystical founder
of the Sufis—Tammuz, and St. George are simply one and
the same person portrayed in a varying mythological guise.
Tammuz has been described as the spouse, son, or brother
of the goddess Ishtar and is known as "the Lord of Life and
Death," a title that has deep Masonic overtones and yet
which pre-dates the reputed history of the Masonic
movement by several millennia.

In the window at Rosslyn, St. George is depicted as standing upon a rose-colored board decorated with Roses or Rosettes, which used to decorate the temples of Ishtar and Tammuz. Longinus and Mauritius are shown standing on a black and white chessboard, the "Checker-board of Joy," symbolizing the Templar battle flag, the "Beauséante," the mystical "hopscotch" symbol of the Pilgrimage of Initiation from Santiago of Compostela to Rosslyn and the ritual floor covering of modern Masonic temples.

Tammuz gives us a strong indication of the origins of the Green Man. Each May, in England, the May Queen was drawn on a cart through the streets by young men and women. Her partner or, in some traditions, her son, was the Green Man clothed in leaves. Ishtar was also known as "the widow," and Tammuz as "the son of the widow." His annual death each Fall and his rebirth each spring symbolized death to the things of the material world for the true initiate and rebirth to the higher realms of the spiritual life.

Understanding the symbolism within Rosslyn Chapel leads to the inevitable conclusion that it was created to transmit Templar and Rex Deus teaching to future generations. Earl William used the skills of his Masonic colleagues to celebrate every known initiatory spiritual pathway that contributed to the sacred Gnosis preserved at such cost by the descendants of the 24 *ma'madot* of Israel. This was not the only means used by Earl William to ensure the preservation of these initiatory rites. Sacred principles central to the Rex Deus tradition have been used for over 500 years by a fraternity that was profoundly influenced, if not founded, by Earl William, for he used the construction of this holy shrine as the first step in the creation of an organization that would treasure and guard these secrets, and pass them on to future generations throughout the world—the craft of Freemasonry.

STAINED GLASS WINDOW DEPICTING ST. MAURITIUS, ONE OF THE LEGENDARY HOLDERS OF THE SPEAR OF DESTINY, THE CLERESTORY, ROSSLYN CHAPEL.

embryonic freemasonry

UNDER THE GUIDANCE OF REX DEUS, THE MEDIEVAL CRAFTMASONS BEGIN TO
EVOLVE INTO THE MODERN CRAFT OF FREEMASONRY, INCORPORATING MANY OF
THE IDEALS OF RENAISSANCE THINKING.

During the Renaissance, the Rex Deus families exerted a profound influence upon individuals who, at first glance, seem unlikely prospects for their attention: Sandro Filipepi, better known as Botticelli, was a Hermetic and a pupil of Verrocchio, the master who instructed Leonardo da Vinci. Leonardo's historical reputation as an esotericist is well known: he is described both as a Rosicrucian and as having a heretical cast of mind. Robert Fludd, author of one of the most comprehensive compilations of ancient hermetic philosophy ever written, was also allegedly a Rosicrucian and one of the principal scholars responsible for the translation of the Authorized Version of the Bible. The priest and alchemist Johann Valentin Andrea was a Rosicrucian of note and the author of the Rosicrucian Manifestos in the mid-seventeenth century. However, these were not the only people selected by the Rex Deus families for instruction in their teachings.

Before and during the construction of Rosslyn Chapel, certain members were carefully selected from operative craft guilds for instruction in the sacred knowledge of science, geometry, history, philosophy, and the secret teachings of Rex Deus. As a result, Scotland—and Midlothian in particular—became a beacon of equity and enlightenment, for this new brotherhood of speculative "free" masons created charitable institutions to support the poorer members of society, and their respective guilds also set money aside for the benefit of their less fortunate brethren. These were the first charitable institutions to be established in Scotland outside the control of the Catholic Church. Indeed, they may well have been the first such benevolent organizations in Europe.

The foundation of Rosslyn Chapel led to the assembling of a large group of masons from every part of Europe which gave Earl William the opportunity to develop this type of organization. His position as hereditary Grand Master of all

CHARITABLE MASONS

THE EARLY FREEMASONS CREATED THE FIRST CHARITABLE INSTITUTIONS IN SCOTLAND THAT WERE OUTSIDE THE CONTROL OF THE CHURCH AND WHICH MAY WELL HAVE BEEN THE FIRST BENEVOLENT INSTITUTIONS ESTABLISHED IN EUROPE.

the guilds in Scotland, his authority over the Masonic court at Kilwinning, and the Masonic symbolism within Rosslyn Chapel, demonstrate that he had the means, the motive, and the opportunity to play a formative and influential role in transforming the craft guilds into the precursor of modern, speculative Freemasonry. This newly emerging fraternity recognized no barriers of class, and eventually even included King James VI of Scotland who was initiated into the craft at the Lodge of Perth and Scone in 1601. When he became King James I of England two years later, he needed influential allies as a counterweight to the power of the self-serving British aristocracy, and he found them among the trade and craft guilds of England whom he introduced to Freemasonry. The earliest documentary proof of initiations into Freemasonry in England date from 1640, during the reign of his son, King Charles I.

The innate secrecy of early Freemasonry poses almost insuperable difficulties to those evaluating the full spectrum of esoteric streams that coalesced to form the fraternity, and erects barriers that prevent us from gaining an accurate understanding of the circumstances in each country that influenced local and national developments. In Scotland, the craft had a democratic appeal from the very beginning and has continued in this manner ever since. There, the tradition of preserving the sacred Gnosis in an ascending hierarchy of degrees was kept intact with considerable sophistication. This led ultimately to the development of the Royal Arch degrees of Scottish Freemasonry and, as a result of later developments in France, to Scottish Rite Freemasonry, which is still preserved in a relatively pure form in parts of Europe and the United States. In Europe, Freemasonry developed an

KING JAMES VI OF SCOTLAND, INITIATED INTO THE CRAFT AT THE LODGE OF PERTH AND SCONE IN 1601, WHO, WHEN HE BECAME

KING JAMES I OF ENGLAND, INTRODUCED THE TRADE AND CRAFT GUILDS OF ENGLAND TO FREEMASONRY.

The inherently democratic traditions of the Scottish craft exerted a deep and lasting influence on emerging American Freemasonry, which tends to explain the high quality of the attainments of members on the new continent. These men possessed great spiritual insight and a moral force that became public in the form of the Constitution of the United States of America. This ringing endorsement of freedom, democracy, and the rights of man is the true and lasting spiritual legacy of this branch of Freemasonry, for many of those who created and signed the American Constitution were either Freemasons or Rosicrucians, including George Washington, Benjamin Franklin, Thomas Jefferson, John Adams, and Charles Thompson.

Medieval alchemical practices found their way into American culture using symbols such as the eagle, olive branch, arrows, pentagrams, truncated pyramid, and the all-seeing "eye of Horus" that decorate American banknotes, buildings and monuments—all of them pointers to the influence of the mystical fraternity of Freemasonry on American life.

REX DEUS IN MASONIC RITUAL

There are certain correspondences between Masonic ritual and Rex Deus tradition that are readily identifiable. For example, the Rex Deus oath of secrecy, "Lest my throat be

inherent anticlerical and anti-Catholic bias, and for the first two or three centuries maintained close links with its Scottish brethren, both those at home and those of the Jacobite persuasion living in exile. According to the records of the Rite of Strict Observance, Masons from operative lodges of the Compagnonnage in France visited a craft lodge in Aberdeen as early as 1361, beginning a relationship that continued for several centuries therafter. French lodges today take great pains to preserve the original esoteric teaching of the craft as far as possible. In England, on the other hand, once Freemasonry had allied itself to the House of Hanover, the anticlerical bias almost vanished, and English Freemasonry began to be perceived as an integral part of the Church/state establishment.

cut or my tongue cut out," has a parallel in the ritual of the first craft degree of Freemasonry:

These several points I solemnly swear to observe, without evasion, equivocation or mental reservation of any kind under no less a penalty than to have my throat cut across, my tongue torn out by the root and my body buried in the rough sands of the sea at low water mark.

The phrase, "Or let my heart be torn or cut out of my chest," which is the second part of the penalty of the Rex Deus oath, has its equivalent in Freemasonry's second degree:

under no less a penalty than to have my left breast cut open, my heart torn there from, and given to the ravenous birds of the air, or to the devouring beasts of the field as prey.

Two other replications of the Rex Deus oath are found in Masonic ritual: "Or let my eyes be plucked out" is rendered in the ritual of the Knight White Eagle as "under the penalty of forever remaining in perpetual darkness."

The use of a knife as a threat in the oath is replicated in the penalties listed for the Past Master degree:

having my hands lopped off at the wrist and my arms struck from my body and both hung at my breast suspended at the neck as a sign of infamy till time and putridity consume the same.

The support of English Freemasonry for the Hanoverian dynasty led, ultimately, to the United Grand Lodge of England's actively discouraging serious investigation into the true origins of the craft, because they wished to delete references to its Scottish origins and its alliance with the Stuart cause. So there was a purging of many Scottish rituals from English Masonic practice, but, thanks to the Masonic scholar Dimitrije Mitrinovic, many of these rituals have been recorded and clear Rex Deus influence can be discerned within them.

One of these degrees, that of the Secret Master, is concerned with mourning for someone who remains anonymous. This degree commemorates an era when the building of the Herodian Temple in Jerusalem was halted due to a tragedy. For this ritual the lodge is draped in black and white and illuminated by the light of 81 candles. The jewel of the degree is inscribed with the letter "z," which refers to Zadok—and in the Dead Sea Scrolls we discover that the sons of Zadok were the descendants of the high priests of the Temple who were also known as "the Righteous Seed" or "the Sons of Dawn." This refers directly to

James the Just, who succeeded Jesus in the position of the Zadok, or "Teacher of Righteousness."

THE LEGEND OF HIRAM ABIF

Craft tradition claims that Freemasonry arose at the time of King Solomon when Hiram Abif was killed by a blow to the temple for his refusal to betray a secret, which again echoes the recorded details of the death of James the Just, who was killed by a blow to the temple with a fuller's club. Hiram

PURGING OF MASONIC RITUAL

AFTER THE ACCESSION OF THE HANOVERIAN DYNASTY, THE GRAND LODGE OF ENGLAND TRIED TO PURGE MASONIC RITUAL OF ALL REFERENCES TO THE SCOTTISH ORIGINS OF THE CRAFT AND ITS EARLIER REX DEUS HERETICAL ROOTS.

was allegedly killed prior to the completion of Solomon's Temple, yet, almost 1,000 years later, when work on the Herodian Temple was nearing completion, building was brought to a halt as a mark of respect for James, the brother of Jesus, who had just been ritually murdered. The Masonic historians Chris Knight and Robert Lomas claim that the tradition concerning the death of Hiram Abif is simply an allegory for the murder of James the Just. If this is true, and it may well be, when Freemasons celebrate the death of Hiram Abif they are commemorating one of the most important early members of Rex Deus.

Another suppressed degree, that of the Perfect Master, supposedly commemorates the reburial of the corpse of Hiram, and in this ritual the lodge is lit by four groups of four candles, each placed at the cardinal points of the compass. The ritual recounts that King Solomon ordered Adoniram to build a tomb for Hiram Abif in the form of an obelisk of black-and-white marble, the entrance being between two pillars supporting a square lintel engraved with the letter. "J." The association between this degree and the death of James the Just is thus made absolutely explicit, and

furthermore, in this degree the lodge is draped in green. Green and gold are the heraldic colors of the royal house of David, one of the Rex Deus families. Green and gold occur again as part of the fifteenth degree, that of the Knight of the Sword and the Knight of the East, which celebrates the building of Zerubabel's Temple. It is strange that at Rosslyn, a place of such importance to Freemasonry, with so many references to the building of Zerubabel's Temple, there is yet no direct reference to Solomon's Temple, only individual carvings of items described in the Bible as being within the Temple.

The founding of the Rex Deus military arm, the Knights Templar, is also celebrated in one of the suppressed degrees: that of the Knight of the East and West. This ritual claims that the degree was first created in 1118, when eleven knights took vows of secrecy, fraternity, and discretion under the aegis of the patriarch of Jerusalem. The knights included all nine founders of the Templars with, in addition, Count Fulk d'Anjou and Count Hughes I of Champagne. The presiding officer is known as the Most Equitable Most Sovereign Prince Master, who is supported by the High Priest. Authors Knight and Lomas suggest that the Most Equitable Most Sovereign Prince Master was originally King Baldwin II of Jerusalem, and it may well be that the High Priest in this ritual represents the cousin of Bernard of Clairvaux, who was patriarch of Jerusalem.

The twentieth degree, that of Grand Master—yet another that was suppressed—describes the destruction of the second Temple in Jerusalem by the Romans in 70 CE, tells of the grief experienced by the brethren who were in the Holy Land, and further recounts how they had to flee from their homeland with the intention of erecting a third Temple that would be a spiritual rather than a physical edifice. For all Freemasons, the creation of this new spiritual Temple of God on Earth has become a sacred duty. The ritual continues

THE DEATH OF HIRAM ABIF, SAID TO BE AN ALLEGORY FOR THE MURDER OF JAMES THE JUST, JESUS' SUCCESSOR.

with the story of how the brethren divided themselves into a number of lodges before scattering throughout the length and breadth of Europe. One came to Scotland and established itself at Kilwinning, where it was charged with the sacred duty of keeping the records of their Order. Thus the ritual tells the story of the scattering of the original Rex Deus families.

Encoding such Rex Deus traditions in a variety of degrees within the traditions of Freemasonry is very much like a man on the run seeking refuge in a crowded city. It is also similar to the manner used by Earl William St. Clair, who hid a plethora of Templar and Rex Deus symbolism among a host of apparently confusing carvings within Rosslyn Chapel. Despite the vigorous attempts of the Hanoverian censors to extinguish all knowledge of these degrees, they have nonetheless been recorded for posterity and indeed may well still be in use elsewhere. What they do prove beyond all doubt is that the Rex Deus families were indeed the

prime movers in the creation of Freemasonry, and intended this fact to be recorded within the Craft.

ANOTHER THEORY OF EARLY DEVELOPMENT

Following the suppression of the Templars, the rapid disappearance of so many Knights was seemingly inexplicable until fairly recently. The American Masonic historian John Robinson claimed that the Templars had used a previously unsuspected organization, the Craftmasons, as a vehicle for their escape. Robinson gives a plausible explanation for the secret rituals and greetings of the Freemasons, claiming that Freemasonry was developed as a direct consequence of the Craftmasons aiding Templar Knights fleeing from persecution. His work also tends to confirm that there were some tenuous links between the Templar Order in Scotland and early Freemasonry.

The mystery that surrounds the foundation of Freemasonry has been further clouded by the inescapable fact that each craft guild in medieval Europe had its own—sometimes very different—foundation myth, traditions, and rituals. The debate about how and where the Craftmasons were transformed into the precursors of modern Freemasonry has been prolonged and bitter, and this has complicated any rational study of the issue. Debate over Masonic origins, even within the Craft, has often degenerated into a modern version of *odium theologicum*, in which the character of the proponents is questioned more vigorously than their theories. It is a fact that one family above all others had the means, the motive, and the opportunity to exert a transformative effect on the medieval craft guilds of operative masons and to use them to such good effect that they developed into the founders of the modern craft of speculative Freemasonry. But this statement of the strong possibility will not silence those who vigorously defend their pro- or anti-Templar theories of

AN EIGHTEENTH-CENTURY REPRESENTATION OF ONE OF THE THIRD-DEGREE INITIATION RITUALS, MOST PROBABLY FROM THE GRAND ORIENT OF FRANCE.

origin. It is hoped that serious investigation of the matter will eventually provide the essential keys that resolve this historical conundrum for all time.

THE ON-GOING DEVELOPMENT OF FREEMASONRY

The secrecy of the Craft and the paucity of records documenting its early years make the task of accurately tracing its diverse origins extremely difficult. It is a problem exacerbated by the habit of describing the fraternity as a worldwide brotherhood when it is in reality a varied collection of differing Orders and jurisdictions with their own rituals, which sometimes differ widely from one another. Nonetheless, these seemingly differing brotherhoods do have a common root, and furthermore the aims and objectives of each of them display a startling similarity. Freemasonry claims to be a fraternity founded upon the principles of brotherhood, charity, and truth, within which its members aspire to attain standards of morality and spirituality taught by means of allegory and ritual. This initiatory manner of teaching is a derivative of the Rex Deus tradition. The Craft's main purpose is to help each member to perfect himself so that he can serve society at large, and this objective echoes the ethos of the Knights Templar and even earlier Egyptian initiatory principles. It also replicates the aim of the Sons of Zadok, the Essenes, whose purpose was to create an élite within the élite, who would then act as an example to all of Israel so that Israel would become a "light unto the Gentiles."

The manner of instruction uses the symbolism of the tools of the earlier Craftmasons, such as the square, compasses, rule, plumb line, mallet, and chisels. Each new initiate is encouraged to apply these tools and work on the rough stone of his own being in order to re-shape himself into the perfect "ashlar of enlightenment" so that he can build the Temple of God on Earth in a spiritual form. These tools are thus used to knock off the rough edges of the "stone" and create an improved and highly moral being, and in this manner the process of initiation into the degrees of Freemasonry replicates, albeit in different allegorical terms, the alchemical process of transmuting the base metal of humanity into the pure gold of spiritual enlightenment.

consolidation and division

FREEMASONRY ADOPTS A BAN ON THE DISCUSSION OF BOTH RELIGION AND POLITICS, AND UNDER ROYAL PATRONAGE FLOURISHES AT FIRST, ONLY TO SUFFER DIVISIONS THAT STILL INFLUENCE THE CRAFT TODAY.

ELIAS ASHMOLE

Life in Europe at the end of the sixteenth century was very different from the life people there experience today. Each of its kingdoms was subject to rigid social and class divisions and in many, including England, social division was exacerbated by bitter religious disputes—for not far below the surface of an apparently stable society in England there simmered considerable religious division and distrust nurturing the seeds of conflict. Protestants had been burned at the stake as martyrs in the reign of Queen Mary, and Catholics were almost perpetually suspected of plotting against the throne. Thus it was that in the reign of King Charles I, the son of the first Stuart monarch King James I of England, civil war broke out. It was a battle for political supremacy between the King and Parliament, made worse by the suspicion that the King had Catholic sympathies and exacerbated by the strict Puritan and Protestant ideals of many of the Parliamentarians. The war ultimately resulted in the execution of the King and the rule of the Puritan Oliver Cromwell, who instituted the "Commonwealth." In this war, brother fought against brother, aristocrats fought on both sides, and the common people, Catholic and Protestant alike, suffered greatly. It was at the height of this brutal and divisive civil war that the initiation of one of England's most famous early Freemasons took place.

Elias Ashmole was a scholar and a Royalist who was captured by Parliamentary forces. Placed under house arrest by his captors, Ashmole, having given his parole, was billeted with his father-in-law, a staunch supporter of the Parliamentary cause. A lodge was specially formed to initiate Brother Elias Ashmole and, surprisingly, it was drawn from Masons who were a mixed group of Royalists and Parliamentarians. This was possible because Freeemasonry, from its very beginnings, was a fraternity in which the discussion of both religion and politics was strictly forbidden. True brotherly love, or tolerance, to use a common expression, stresses the similarities that bind men together and not the differences that tend to separate them. Thus, in the earliest records it is evident that the fraternity of Freemasonry was a brotherhood dedicated to a belief in God and the three great principles of brotherly love, charity, and truth. Freemasons of that time, however, were not the only men who wished to bring an end to religious and political strife, nor were they alone in wishing to meet in harmony and work for the betterment of society.

The mysterious Order known as the Rosicrucians certainly existed before Freemasonry came to public attention. Its followers formed an "invisible college" of like-minded, spiritually enlightened men, and its influence—even in the twenty-first century—is reckoned by many to be profound. Many of the formative figures throughout the seventeenth and eighteenth centuries admitted to Rosicrucian influences in their thinking. They became known as "the Invisibles." Their immediate spiritual ancestors were most probably the society known as the *orden der Unzertrennlichen* or *"Indissolubisten."* Founded in 1577 it included owners and craftsmen smelters among its membership. Surprisingly, alchemy was their foremost interest. An indication of the belief of certain seventeenth-century Masons in the putative Templar origins of the Craft can be found in the translation of Heinrich Cornelius Agrippa's *Of Occult Philosophy,* which was first published in English in 1651. The original Latin version contained a phrase that reads "the detestable heresy of the Templars"; in the English translation this becomes transcribed as "the detestable heresy of old churchmen."

Others claim that a variety of initiates combined in an international network with moderate scholars in the tradition of Erasmus to form the "Third Force," a movement of moderation created to combat the excesses of both Catholics and protestants—a group who, in cooperation with the Dutch esoteric movement known as the "Family of Love," formed the "Invisible College" whose members were in constant correspondence with one another. It was such a college that, under the guidance of leading English Freemasons, eventually came into the open when they founded the Royal Society in England.

ELIAS ASHMOLE, THE RENOWNED SCHOLAR, WHO WAS INITIATED INTO FREEMASONRY DURING THE CIVIL WAR IN A SPECIALLY CONVENED LODGE WHOSE MEMBERSHIP WAS DRAWN FROM BOTH THE PARLIAMENTARY FORCES AND THE ROYALISTS.

The Royal Society was formed by a group of scientists who included the Freemasons Elias Ashmole, Dr. John Wilkins and Sir Robert Moray, all men of profound religious conviction, yet who were so embarrassed by the restrictions placed upon the advance of knowledge by religion that they dedicated their meetings purely to scientific matters and banned all discussion of religion at them. This was of course in replication of one of the basic tenets of Freemasonry; furthermore, it has been suggested—and with good cause—that this was as much to protect the fledgling society from religious persecution and repression as to advance the cause of scientific debate. Thus was born a lasting and valued heir to Masonic tradition, a society that would help lay the foundations for the advancement of science and the development of the modern world. At about the same time as the foundation of the Royal Society by English Freemasons, the Holy Mother Church placed Galileo under house arrest and forbade him to publish the results of his research. The stark contrast between the Masonic attitude to learning and that of the Church was to be repeated in later centuries in their respective attitudes to democracy.

During the brief era of the Commonwealth, while Cromwell ruled England and Prince Charles, who later became King Charles II, was in exile in Holland, some Masonic lodges in England stayed in communication with him. Acting as an informed quasi-intelligence service, his Masonic brothers kept the exiled Prince fully informed of political developments in England. Some authorities claim that after his restoration it was as an act of gratitude to these lodges that he became patron of the Royal Society,

BELOW: KING CHARLES I, DURING WHOSE REIGN WAS FOUGHT THE ENGLISH CIVIL WAR. NOMINALLY A PROTESTANT, CHARLES WAS SUSPECTED OF HAVING CATHOLIC SYMPATHIES. HE WAS EXECUTED ON JANUARY 30, 1649.

RIGHT: DR. JOHN WILKINS, A NOTED FREEMASON WHO, ALONG WITH OTHER MEMBERS OF THE CRAFT SUCH AS ELIAS ASHMOLE AND SIR ROBERT MORAY, HELPED TO FOUND THE ROYAL SOCIETY.

King George I enter'd London most magnificently on 20th September 1724. And, after the rebellion was over — AD 1716 — the few Lodges at London ... thought fit to cement themselves under a Grand Master as the centre of union and harmony, viz. the Lodges that met:

1. *at the Goose and Gridiron Ale-house in St Paul's churchyard*
2. *at the Crown Ale-house in Parker's Lane near Drury Lane*
3. *at the Appletree Tavern in Charles Street, Covent Garden*
4. *at the Runner and Grape Tavern in Channel-Row, Westminster*

They and some other old Brothers met at the said Appletree, and having put in the chair the oldest Master-Mason, they constituted themselves a Grand Lodge pro Tempore in Due Form, and forthwith revived the Quarterly Communication of the Officers of Lodges (called the Grand Lodge), resolved to hold the Annual Assembly and Feast, and then to chuse a Grand Master from among themselves, till they should have a Noble Brother at their Head.

which they had been instrumental in founding. However, when the Stuarts were deposed and ultimately replaced by the Hanoverian dynasty, this earlier alliance between some Freemasons and the Stuarts became an acute cause of anxiety to the Craft in England, and as a result the number of lodges and the total overall membership suffered a severe decline. This situation became appreciably worse after the defeat of the Scottish rebellion in 1715. A witch-hunt took place in England of which any supposed Jacobite supporters were the targets. At this time many Masons left the Craft with considerable haste. If Freemasonry was to continue in England, it had to change radically and divest itself of any vestige of Jacobite sympathy or pride in its Scottish origins.

The revised *Book of Constitutions* written by Dr. James Anderson in 1738 discloses that, in 1716, only four lodges remained in being, and they had immediately to manifest their loyalty to King George I. Anderson records that:

The use of the word "revived" implies that some of these "new" issues had been standard practice at one time but had since fallen into disuse. However, the paucity of records that bedevils all who investigate the history of Freemasonry makes it impossible to prove or disprove this assertion. Their loyalist intentions were made explicit by their expressed desire to have "a Noble Brother at their Head." This, of course, was nothing new. King James I of England had been their titular head a century earlier and the new "Grand Lodge" was simply avowing its intention of drawing its next head from the Hanoverian dynasty. Anderson, in his revised *Book of Constitutions*, invented an imaginative and inaccurate version of Masonic history that was deliberately designed to distance the Craft from its true Scottish origins. He alleged that English Freemasonry had begun in York during the reign of King Athelstan with an assembly of Masons convened by Prince Edwin in 926, a theory later

RIGHT: THE DUKE OF MONTAGUE, THE FIRST NOBLEMAN TO BE ELECTED GRAND MASTER OF THE GRAND LODGE IN LONDON IN 1721 AND WHOSE LEADERSHIP BEGAN TO BE RECOGNIZED BY LODGES OUTSIDE OF LONDON.

FAR RIGHT: EIGHTEENTH-CENTURY ILLUSTRATION OF A FRENCH MASON OF THE SCOTTISH RITE, WEARING TEMPLAR REGALIA.

supported by Robert Graves. Meanwhile, the Grand Lodge continued to develop: in 1721 the Duke of Montague became its first noble Grand Master and lodges outside of London began to recognize its authority. By 1730 it had taken more than 100 lodges under its wing and began to exercise a supervisory role, appointing Provincial Grand Masters to both superintend provincial lodges and stimulate interest in Freemasonry throughout the country. Furthermore, it began to export Freemasonry to foreign parts and issued dispensations or warrants to constitute lodges in Spain and India.

It would appear that at least one lodge existed in Ireland by 1688, most probably at Trinity College, Dublin. The records of the early years of Freemasonry in Ireland sadly have been lost; however, a newspaper report in the *Dublin Weekly Journal* records that the Grand Master and Grand Officers with representatives from six Dublin lodges met to elect new Grand Lodge officers, so the first Irish Grand Lodge must have preceded the publication of this article on June 26, 1725. Another Grand Lodge was founded in Munster in 1726, and the two Grand Lodges were merged in 1731. Scotland formed its first Grand Lodge in 1736.

The Grand Lodge of Scotland resulted from a meeting of the Masters and Wardens of Scottish lodges held at Mary's Chapel on the November 30, 1736. We do not know with any degree of certainty how many lodges existed in Scotland at that time, but only 32 were represented at that important meeting. The St. Clairs of Roslin were the hereditary Grandmasters of the Guilds of Scotland. Then, on that fateful St. Andrew's Day in 1736, Sir William St. Clair of Roslin formally resigned his "hereditary patronage and protectorship of the Masonic craft" to effect the creation of "The Grand Lodge of Ancient, Free and Accepted Masons of Scotland." The minutes of the meeting disclose that:

... William St. Clair, Earl of Orkney and Caithness, Baron of Roslin, &c., &c., got a grant of this office from King James II. He countenanced the Lodges with his presence, propagated the royal art, and built the chapel of Roslin, that master-piece of Gothic architecture. Masonry now began to spread its benign influence through the country, and many noble and stately buildings were reared by the Prince and Nobles during the time of Grand Master Roslin. By another deed of the said King James II, this office was made hereditary to the said William St. Clair, and his heirs and successors in the Barony of Roslin; in which noble family it has continued without any interruption till of late years. . . .

William St. Clair, of Roslin, Esq. (a real Mason, and a gentleman of the greatest candour and benevolence, inheriting his predecessors' virtues without their fortune), was obliged to dispone the estate: and, having no children of his own, was loth that the office of Grand Master, now vested in his person, should become vacant at his death; . . . as hereditary Grand Master over all

Scotland, he had called this meeting, in order to condescend on a proper plan for electing of a Grand Master; and that in order to promote so laudable a design, he proposed to resign into the hands of the Brethren, or whomsoever they should be pleased to elect, all right, claim, or title whatever, which he or his successors have to reign as Grand Master over the Masons in Scotland . . .

It is claimed that, Sir William's resignation as Grand Master having been reluctantly accepted, the assembled brothers decided:

. . . they could not confer that high honour upon any Brother better qualified, or more properly entitled, than William St. Clair, of Roslin, Esq., whose ancestors had so long presided over the Brethren, and had ever acquitted themselves with honour and with dignity. Accordingly, by a unanimous voice, William St. Clair, of Roslin, Esq., was proclaimed Grand Master Mason of all Scotland, and being placed in the chair, was installed, saluted, homaged, and acknowledged as such.

This somewhat sanitized and diplomatic account tends to disguise the fact, as modern Masonic researchers into this event have discovered, that the election was in all probability rigged. Be that as it may, it is a matter of record that Sir William served in his "new" post with considerable distinction.

Meanwhile, across the border, the apparent authority of the Grand Lodge of England was challenged in 1751 when a rival Grand Lodge, calling itself the Antients Grand Lodge, arose in London. Apparently formed mainly of Irish Masons who claimed that the original Grand Lodge had departed from old and revered practices by altering the rituals, the Antients Grand Lodge soon became a formidable rival to the Grand Lodge of England. Relations between the two rivals were far from fraternal. Neither recognized the other; each erected rival lodges both at home and in foreign parts; and the Antients soon established fraternal correspondence with both the Grand Lodge of Ireland and the Grand Lodge of Scotland. The Antients also created a novel habit that was of incalculable benefit in spreading Freemasonry throughout the British Empire: the granting of traveling warrants to

regimental lodges within the British Army. Freemasonry thus went wherever the regiment was stationed, whether in England, the North American colonies, or India. The split between the Grand Lodge of England and the Antients was to be the first of many schisms in a movement pledged to promote fraternity.

A further complication arose in 1761 when yet another lodge, in York, claimed to be the Grand Lodge of all England. This potentially disastrous situation was not resolved until the two major Grand Lodges eventually united in 1813 under the title of the United Grand Lodge of England.

In Europe, the situation at first moved more slowly and there is little evidence that Freemasonry, as we now know it, existed much before 1720. However, by the 1730s lodges had been established in France, Germany, Belgium, Holland, and Spain, with another in Florence in Italy. The Italian members of the Florence lodge soon attracted the unwelcome attentions of the Inquisition, and before long that lodge was virtually restricted to foreign membership. Jacobite exiles had managed to erect a lodge in Rome somewhat earlier. Freemasonry spread in Europe as a consequence of the appointment of Provincial Grand Masters by the Grand Lodge of England. At first, however, Freemasonry was slow to take root in France and was only used by a small number of aristocrats to further their explorations into esoteric matters, as membership of a society that claimed descent from the medieval stonemasons held little attraction for the French middle class or the intellectuals of that time. That was soon to change in a dramatic manner that would influence political, cultural, and social developments not merely within France but throughout the world. This came about as the result of a speech made not by a Frenchman but by a Scots Jacobite exile—the man known to history as Chevalier Ramsay.

ANTIENTS GRAND LODGE AND
WALL OF LODGE SIGNS, FROM
THE EIGHTEENTH CENTURY.

the human catalyst

ANOTHER REMARKABLE SCOTSMAN TRANSFORMS FREEMASONRY, BUT THIS TIME
IN FRANCE. CHEVALIER RAMSAY OPENS THE DOOR TO FRENCH INTELLECTUALS
AND ARISTOCRATS BY EMPHASIZING THE CRAFT'S CRUSADER HERITAGE.

Freemasonry, as it spread across the English Channel with English diplomats, received a massive boost when the deposed Stuart King James II arrived in France accompanied by a large entourage of Scottish Jacobite Freemasons. Masonry began to spread throughout the continent among the various English and Scottish expatriate communities. This was in stark contrast to the reactions of the French people themselves who, apart from a very small number of aristocrats interested in esoteric studies, proved supremely reluctant to join an organization that claimed descent from simple Craftmasons. This was soon to change dramatically as a result of one rather controversial man.

CHEVALIER RAMSAY

Andrew Michael Ramsay (1681–1743) graduated from Edinburgh University and then, like so many others, became involved in the bitter religious disputes that tore Scotland apart during the first ten years of the eighteenth century. As a result, he fled to France in 1710, eventually converted to Catholicism, and then took employment under the patronage of the Duc de Chateau-Thierry, before working for the Prince de Turenne. In return for these services to the nobility he was rewarded by being made a knight of the Order of St. Lazarus, thereby becoming Chevalier Ramsay, a name of considerable note to Masonic historians. Ramsay traveled to Rome in 1724 to act as tutor to Prince Charles Edward Stuart. Being something of an eccentric character, albeit a staunch Jacobite, he was not well liked by the Prince, however, and his employment as the royal tutor lasted less than a year.

On his return to Paris, Ramsay—a university graduate, a fellow of the Royal Society, one-time tutor to Bonnie Prince Charlie, and Grand Chancellor of the Paris Grand Lodge—was clearly deemed to have authority and credibility of the highest order. He is remembered for an oration presented to

PRINCE CHARLES EDWARD STUART, MORE POPULARLY KNOWN AS "BONNIE PRINCE CHARLIE" OR "THE YOUNG PRETENDER," THE LEADER OF THE REBELLION OF 1745 AGAINST THE HANOVERIAN DYNASTY.

RAMSAY'S THEORY OF ORIGIN

"OUR FOUNDERS WERE NOT SIMPLE WORKERS IN STONE ... BUT ALSO RELIGIOUS AND WARRIOR PRINCES WHO DESIGNED TO ENLIGHTEN, EDIFY AND PROTECT THE LIVING TEMPLES OF THE MOST HIGH."

the Masonic Lodge of St. Thomas in Paris on March 21, 1737. This speech, which was widely circulated, stimulated a massive influx of new adherents to Freemasonry in France, for the Chevalier announced to the world that, far from having its origins among the unlettered masons of the medieval era, Freemasonry had been founded by a consortium of the kings, princes, knights, and nobility at the time of the Crusades. His speech, which is one of the most important in the history of Freemasonry, included the following passages:

The noble ardour which you, gentlemen, evince to enter into the most noble and very illustrious Order of Freemasons, is a certain proof that you already possess all the qualities necessary to become members—that is humanity, pure morals, inviolable secrecy, and a taste for the fine arts. ...

Our ancestors, the Crusaders, gathered together from all parts of Christendom in the Holy Land, desired thus to reunite into one sole Fraternity the individuals of all nations. What obligations do we not owe to these superior men who, without gross selfish interests, without even listening to the inborn tendency to dominate, imagined such an Institution, the sole aim of which is to unite minds and hearts in order to make them better, and form in the course of ages a spiritual empire where, without derogating from the various duties which different States exact, a new people shall be created, which, composed of many nations, shall in some sort cement them all into one by the ties of virtue and science? ...

The word "Freemason" must therefore not be taken in a literal, gross, and material sense, as if our founders had been simple workers in stone, or merely curious geniuses who wished to perfect the arts. They were not only skillful architects, desirous of consecrating their talents and goods to the construction of material temples; but also religious and warrior princes who designed to enlighten, edify, and protect the living Temples of the Most High. This I will demonstrate by developing the history or rather the renewal of the Order. ...

At the time of the Crusades in Palestine many princes, lords, and citizens associated themselves, and vowed to restore the Temple of the Christians in the Holy Land, and to employ themselves in bringing back their architecture to its first institution. They agreed upon several ancient signs and symbolic words drawn from the well of religion in order to recognize themselves amongst the heathen and Saracens. These signs and words were only communicated to those who promised solemnly, and even sometimes at the foot of the altar, never to reveal them. This sacred promise was therefore not an execrable oath, as it has been called, but a respectable bond to unite Christians of all nationalities in one confraternity. Sometime afterwards our Order formed an intimate union with the Knights of Saint John of Jerusalem. From that time our Lodges took the name of Lodges of Saint John. ...

The kings, princes, and lords returned from Palestine to their own lands, and there established divers Lodges. At the time of the last Crusades many Lodges were already erected in Germany, Italy, Spain, France, and from thence in Scotland, because of the close alliance between the French and the Scots. James, Lord Steward of Scotland, was Grand Master of a Lodge established at Kilwinning, in the West of Scotland, 1286, shortly after the death of Alexander III, King of Scotland, and one year before John Baliol mounted the throne. This lord received as Freemasons into his Lodge the Earls of Gloucester and Ulster, the one English, the other Irish.

By degrees our Lodges and our rites were neglected in most places. This is why of so many historians only

those of Great Britain speak of our Order. Nevertheless it preserved its splendor among those Scotsmen to whom the Kings of France confided during many centuries the safeguard of their royal persons.

From the British Isles the Royal Art is now re-passing into France, under the reign of the most amiable of Kings, whose humanity animates all his virtues, and under the ministry of a Mentor who has realized all that could be imagined most fabulous. In his happy age when love of peace has become the virtue of heroes, this nation [France], one of the most spiritual of Europe, will be the centre of the Order. She will clothe our work, our statutes, and our customs with grace, delicacy, and good taste, essential qualities of the Order, of which the basis is the wisdom, strength, and beauty of genius.

Forges à Cornes.

Thus the able Scots orator claimed that the original Freemasons were not illiterate stone-workers but men of nobility who had vowed to rebuild the Temple of God on Earth in the Holy Land, and that the Lord Steward of Scotland became the first Grand Master of the only surviving lodge at Kilwinning in 1286. Scotland therefore was the only country that could honestly claim to have maintained an unbroken line of tradition of the craft of Freemasonry from the end of the Crusades until the present. Furthermore, Ramsay took pains to stress the intellectual pursuits that were an essential part of Freemasonry and stated unequivocally that the spiritual climate of France was the perfect launch-pad for a viable renewal of this ancient and noble art.

The Chevalier's oration was published twice—once in an obscure journal, and then in the *The Almanac des Cocus* in 1741, which gained wide circulation and stimulated considerable interest throughout France. The French middle classes and intellectuals who had been extremely reluctant to join an organization that derived from manual workers now became highly enthusiastic, for a fraternity that was the heir of medieval Chivalric Orders was a very different kettle of fish indeed. Enthusiasm for Freemasonry swept through France, attracting all and sundry who had any pretensions to nobility, chivalry, romance, and spiritual brotherhood. However, according to the English author Laurence Gardner, there was a distinct and substantial difference between the old-style Rosicrucian degree system used by the Jacobite Freemasons in France and the new system of degrees and rituals which, allegedly, only arose following Ramsay's oration and that became known as the Ancient and Accepted Rite with a 33-degree system. This system, despite its name, should not be confused either with that practiced by the Freemasons under the jurisdiction of the Antients Grand Lodge in England or with that of the Ancient Accepted Free Masons of Scotland.

While Ramsay is most certainly not responsible for the invention of the 33-degree system, he certainly gained popularity as a direct consequence of his oration, and it became known as the Scottish Rite to distinguish it from the English rites that were already in use in France following the erection of Lodges there under the aegis of the Grand Lodges in England. Many of these "new" extra degrees imparted a knightly gloss on their holders and were compared by their enthusiastic members to the ancient chivalric Orders they imitated. Nonetheless, true Scottish influence was present, for in true Scots democratic tradition Scottish-rite Freemasonry was established on the fundamental principles laid down in the Declaration of Arbroath in 1310.

ALMANACH

DES

COCUS,

OU

AMUSEMENS
Pour le beau Sexe.

POUR L'ANNE'E M. DCC. XLI.

Auquel on a joint un recueil de Pieces
fur les Francs-Maçons.

Ouvrage Inftructif, Epigrammatique, &
Enigmatique, dedié a la Jeuneffe
amoureufe.

Par un Philofophe Garçon.

A CONSTANTINOPLE,
De l'Imprimerie du GRAND SEIGNEUR

M. DCC. XLI.

Avec Approbation des Sultans.

TITLE PAGE OF THE *ALMANACH DES COCUS*, WHICH PRINTED THE ENTIRE TEXT OF CHEVALIER RAMSAY'S ORATION IN 1741.

Most Masonic historians owing allegiance to the United Grand Lodge of England are highly critical of Ramsay and claim that these "Higher Degrees" are pure invention. However, the validity of this approach is in some doubt because various documents and letters have been found that indicate that the "higher degrees" were in existence before Ramsay delivered his oration. Furthermore, Ramsay had stressed descent from the Order of St. John and nowhere in his oration had mentioned the Knights Templar at all, yet, despite the comments of Laurence Gardner cited above, Templar references and influence predominated in the "new" higher degrees. The Masonic historian Cyril N. Batham rightly concluded that "this is all so confusing," but there is no doubt that Jacobite lodges and the new Scottish rite played a crucial role in publicizing the idea of a strong and distinct Templar heritage permeating Freemasonry.

Ramsay, as a devout Catholic convert, may well have hoped that his oration, with its claim that Freemasonry descended from the Crusaders in general and the Knights of St. John in particular, might make the Order seem acceptable to the papacy. If that was his intent, however, he was mistaken, for in 1738, after the promulgation of yet another anti-Masonic papal bull, *In Eminenti Apostolatus Specula*, which forbade Catholics from joining Freemasonry under pain of excommunication, a copy of Ramsay's oration was publicly burned in Rome. After this, Ramsay seems to have disappeared from the Masonic scene, apparently valuing religious devotion and loyalty to Holy Mother the Church more than his undoubted enthusiasm for the Craft.

THE KNIGHTS TEMPLAR CONNECTION?

The influence of Templar tradition on Freemasonry became even more apparent some years later when the Chevalier de Bérage wrote a pamphlet in 1747 which gave the following account of the origins of Freemasonry:

This Order was instituted by Godefroi de Bouillon in Palestine in 1330, after the decadence of the Christian armies, and was only communicated to the French Masons some time after and to a very small number, as a reward for the obliging services they rendered to several of our English and Scottish Knights, from whom true Masonry is taken. Their Metropolitan Lodge is situated on the Mountain of Heredom where the first Lodge was held in Europe and which exists in all its splendor. The General Council is still held there and it is the seal of the Sovereign Grand Master in office. This mountain is situated between the West and North of Scotland at 60 miles from Edinburgh.

This passage is evidence that the idea of a connection between Crusading Knights and the Lodge of Heredom of Kilwinning was becoming widespread by 1747. A little while later, in 1766, Baron Tschoudy wrote in *Étoile Flamboyante* that the crusading origin of Freemasonry was being taught officially in the lodges. Candidates for initiation were told that several knights who had set forth to rescue the holy places of Palestine from the Saracens "formed an association under the name of Free Masons, thus indicating that their principal desire was the reconstruction of the Temple of Solomon." Furthermore, he went on to say that they adopted certain signs, grips, and passwords as a defense against the Saracens, and finally, echoing Ramsay, that "our Society . . . fraternized on the footing of an Order with the Knights of St. John of Jerusalem, from which it is apparent that the Freemasons borrowed the custom of regarding St. John as the patron of the whole Order in general."

Another much disputed theory of the Templar origins of Freemasonry comes to light when we examine the actions of yet another controversial figure in eighteenth-century Masonic circles in Europe, Baron Karl Gotthelf von Hund. What is the truth, if it can be discerned, that lies behind the story of this controversial and influential man?

BARON VON HUND: THE RITE OF STRICT OBSERVANCE

Baron Karl Gotthelf von Hund is remembered as the apparent founder of rectified Masonry, better known as the

Rite of Strict Observance. According to mainstream Masonic historians who support the claims of the United Grand Lodge of England, he is described as "a Saxon nobleman who was the foremost early propagator of the Templar myth in Freemasonry and an enthusiastic creator of Templar rites." His rite, which took the name Strict Observance to distinguish itself from English Craft Masonry, was founded in 1764 and spread rapidly in the German states. Within this tightly structured and disciplined rite, the brethren were dubbed Knights, pledged themselves to absolute obedience to the commands of von Hund, and indulged in sumptuous ceremonies and gorgeous regalia. This apparent revival of Templarism within Freemasonry was founded on the theory that the original Knights Templar were custodians of the secret doctrines which were the real source of Freemasonry. Von Hund claimed that he had been initiated into the Order by certain "Unknown Superiors," among whom was Bonnie Prince Charlie himself. United Grand Lodge historians, among others, treat von Hund's claims with absolute contempt and cite the fact that Prince Charles Edward Stuart denied any involvement with Freemasonry when questioned about these matters in 1777.

So von Hund is dismissed as a fantasist, apparently with some justice. However, certain facts have come to light as the result of research conducted by Michael Baigent and Richard Leigh that disclose background information to indicate the truth of von Hund's claims and give serious cause to re-evaluate both the status of the baron and of the Rite of Strict Observance. Von Hund had already been a Freemason for many years when he began to advertise his new rite with its claim to Templar origins for the Craft. He asserted that he had been introduced to this form of Templar Freemasonry in 1743 by Lord Clifford, the Earl of Kilmarnock, Charles Radclyffe, Earl of Derwentwater, and an "unknown superior" known only as *eques a penna rubra*, the Knight of the Red Feather. A short time after this initiation, von Hund was introduced to Prince Charles Edward Stuart, whom von Hund assumed, incorrectly, was one of the Unknown Superiors. The grounds used to dismiss von Hund as a charlatan by many of his own contemporaries and some modern historians are that Hund's erroneous

identification of Bonnie Prince Charlie as one of his unknown superiors, and the fact that he had apparently been abandoned by them. However, what his more recent critics do not know, or have wilfully chosen to ignore, is that the identity and fate of all who initiated the baron is now a matter of record.

Two years after von Hund's initiation came the 1745 rebellion of the Scots against the Hanoverian dynasty. After the Battle of Culloden at which the Jacobites were finally crushed, Prince Charles Edward Stuart fled to France and the Earl of Kilmarnock was executed, as was Charles Radclyffe. The identity and the ultimate fate of the Knight of the Red Feather was unknown to most people until Baigent and Leigh published their important Masonic work *The Temple and the Lodge* in 1989. The authors had been granted access to the archive of a group known as the Stella Templum, and had found within that collection of documents a letter that identified the Knight of the Red Feather as Alexander Montgomery, the tenth Earl of Eglington, who was also dead by the time von Hund first promulgated his "new" rite. So von Hund's "desertion" by his unknown superiors came about because of their premature deaths following defeat in the 1745 rebellion. Von Hund was thus telling the truth.

In the aftermath of the crushing defeat of the 1745 rebellion, Jacobite Freemasonry—so intimately linked to the discredited Stuart cause—began to die out. Certain of its rituals, suitably modified by the Grand Lodge of England, survived as "Higher Degrees" offered by the Irish Grand Lodge; others found their way into the Scottish Rite; and some survived within von Hund's Rite of Strict Observance. Thus von Hund's so-called fantasy was actually true and, furthermore, his rite spread throughout Europe and eventually reached the North American colonies, later Canada and the United States of America, where it soon took root and flourished among the Jacobite exiles and deportees who had been forcibly settled there.

As we have seen, in its early years at least Freemasonry had certain distinct political overtones and even today it is often associated in the public mind with exerting profound political influence, which seems to belie its long-term prohibition on the discussion of either religion or politics at lodge meetings. This apparent conflict between the public perception and Freemasonry's own claims can only be resolved by examining in some detail the actions of a variety of Freemasons during the eighteenth and nineteenth centuries.

ENGRAVING OF THE BATTLE OF CULLODEN, APRIL 16, 1746, THE LAST PITCHED BATTLE TO BE FOUGHT ON BRITISH SOIL, AT WHICH THE FORCES OF BONNIE PRINCE CHARLIE WERE BRUTALLY DEFEATED BY AN ENGLISH ARMY LED BY THE DUKE OF CUMBERLAND.

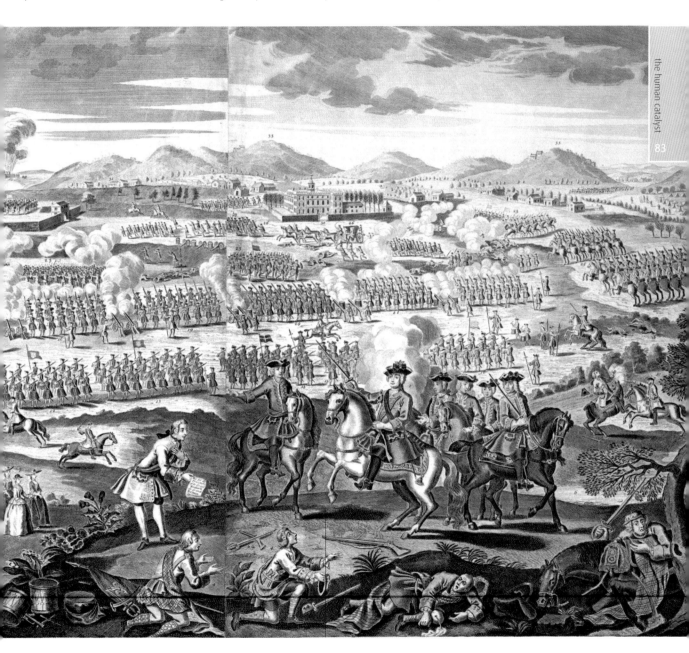

freemasons' influence on society

INDIVIDUAL FREEMASONS HAVE PLAYED A CRITICAL PART IN THE STRUGGLES FOR FREEDOM, NATIONAL INDEPENDENCE, AND DEMOCRACY WORLDWIDE.

o study the formative political and social developments of the eighteenth and nineteenth centuries is to find to our surprise that many leading members of the various movements for change were either Freemasons or men who had been influenced by Freemasonic thought. It is, for these reasons, most probably that the emerging Craft, despite its strictly enforced ban on political and religious discussion within its Lodges, acquired a reputation as being political in nature. Even more controversially, the overt participation of many Masons in the march of progress toward greater democratic involvement and representative government ultimately led to the illusion that membership of the Freemasons was one of the essential keys to political power and commercial success in life.

Indeed, it has often been alleged that the majority of British Prime Ministers and Presidents of the United States of America have been Freemasons. On the back of this sweeping generalization arose the fantasy that Freemasonry as a body was striving toward some vague and unspecified form of world domination. In the rather fevered imagination of conspiracy theorists, both past and present, Freemasonry, acting with politicians of right, left, and center, and allied with the Jews, of course, was trying to establish a "New World Order." Some spurious credence was given to this outrageous theory by the bizarre and shocking events that flowed from the illicit take-over of the Italian Lodge P2 that came to light in the 1980s. The P2 affair was an obscene example of political and financial corruption on a massive scale that allegedly involved the Mafia, the Vatican, and an Italian Bank, the Banco Ambrosiana, which led, in its turn, to the murder of the banker Roberto Calvi in London. This unsavory episode had absolutely nothing to do with the true spirit of Freemasonry or with the Craft as a whole, but was nothing more nor less than a vivid example of the dangers that can arise when unscrupulous individuals take over a branch of a society with closed membership that routinely shrouds its affairs in secrecy.

If, on the other hand, we examine the reality of the involvement of Freemasons in movements of social or democratic progress, the list is truly astounding and includes, among others, the War of American Independence, the creation of the Constitution of the United States, the freeing from oppressive colonial rule of many South American countries, the unification of Italy, and the ending of the temporal and oppressive power of the papacy.

THE AMERICAN WAR OF INDEPENDENCE AND THE FRENCH REVOLUTION

There were, broadly, four ways in which Freemasonry spread beyond the confines of Europe. Firstly, in some places "time immemorial lodges" arose—that is, lodges started at an unknown date by Englishmen who operated without authority from any Grand Lodge or Provincial Master. Benjamin Franklin was first made a Mason in one such self-constituted lodge in Philadelphia as early as 1731. Another way the Freemasons were able to spread so pervasively was that both the Irish Grand Lodge and the Antients Grand Lodge in England issued traveling warrants to army regiments who were then stationed in the colonies. These lodges, which could only operate with the permission of the Colonel of the Regiment concerned, did not simply restrict their membership to soldiers but also initiated civilians, usually the merchants and tradesmen who attended to the regiment's needs. When the regiment was posted elsewhere, many of these local members then founded their own lodge. Thirdly, new arrivals in the colonies who were already Freemasons often applied to the requisite authority or Grand Lodge for a warrant to establish a lodge of their own. The master stroke came when the Grand Lodges of both Scotland and England appointed Provincial Grand Masters for some colonial countries, and this further stimulated the growth of the Craft in parts of the British Empire.

There are many unsubstantiated stories indicating that Freemasonry reached North America with the very earliest colonists in the days long before the establishment of the

ENGRAVING FROM THE FRONTISPIECE OF JAMES ANDERSON'S REVISED *CONSTITUTIONS OF THE FREEMASONS* PUBLISHED IN 1784, DEPICTING TRUTH USING HER MIRROR TO BRING LIGHT TO THE FREEMASONS' HALL. THE OTHER THREE FIGURES ARE FAITH, HOPE, AND CHARITY.

RIGHT: BENJAMIN FRANKLIN, WHO PUBLISHED THE FIRST MASONIC BOOK IN NORTH AMERICA AND DID MUCH TO FACILITATE THE GROWTH OF THE CRAFT THROUGHOUT THE COLONIES.

BELOW: BATTLE OF YORKTOWN. FRENCH GENERAL JEAN DE ROCHAMBEAU AND AMERICAN GENERAL GEORGE WASHINGTON GIVING THE LAST ORDERS FOR THE ATTACK, OCTOBER 1781.

Grand Lodge of England in 1717. There is some evidence to indicate that self-constituted lodges may have existed in Boston and Philadelphia prior to 1730. However it was on June 5 in that year that the Grand Lodge of England appointed David Cox as Provincial Grand Master covering the territories of New York, New Jersey, and Pennsylvania. The appointment of Henry Price as Provincial Grand Master over the ill-defined lands of New England followed on April 13, 1733. With these appointments, the growth of Freemasonry in North America accelerated considerably. The Antients Grand Lodge followed suit, as did both the Grand Lodge of Ireland and the Grand Lodge of Scotland. The end result was that by the outbreak of the American War of Independence there were at least 100 Masonic Lodges established in the British American colonies and some French Lodges further south in Louisiana.

MASONIC HEROES OF THE WAR OF INDEPENDENCE

Benjamin Franklin did a great deal to publicize and promote the growth of Freemasonry on the North American continent. He reported Masonic activities in the local press, reprinted similar articles from British publications, and then became the first American to publish an important Masonic book in the colonies. He printed an edition of Anderson's 1723 *Constitutions,* which is now a much sought-after collector's item and a rarity of great value. In 1755 he assisted in laying the foundation stone for the first purpose-built Masonic building in America, the Masonic Hall in Philadelphia. Franklin spent many years residing in both France and England, and during this prolonged period joined the Nine Sisters Lodge in Paris in 1788, eventually becoming

Master of the Lodge, and was present in that lodge when the French writer Voltaire was initiated into the Craft.

Many of the popular heroes of the American War of Independence were Freemasons, as were many of their opponents. Freemasons numbered among those fighting for independence included, among others, Benjamin Franklin, Paul Revere, John Paul Jones, General Andrew Jackson, the Marquis de Lafayette, and the United States of America's military hero and first president, George Washington.

A great deal of nonsense has been written over the years alleging that the American War of Independence was largely led and fought by Freemasons. Not only is this untrue, it ignores two important matters of fact. The first is that there were as many Freemasons on one side as the other, and the second—perhaps more important—is that it devalues the immense sacrifice and suffering endured by many of the ordinary people involved who had never even heard of the Craft. Yet Freemasonry did play a highly significant part in

the years preceding the conflict in refining the basic principles for which the War was fought and in creating the philosophical basis that was used to found the state that arose after it was concluded.

Freemasonry had wisely forbidden the discussion of both politics and religion at its lodges, but in its attitude of encouraging the study of the seven liberal arts and sciences it created a form of intellectual and philosophical "stock exchange" in which ideas could be both discussed and refined. Middle-class tradesmen, members of the professions, and aristocrats all mixed together in the lodge and discussed and debated new philosophical ideas. The new "enlightenment" and theories of economics all derived from discussing books which many of the members would not normally have heard about, much less read. Furthermore, the idea of government by the consent of the people was inherent in the Declaration of Arbroath which had played such a part in establishing the ambience of true democracy to which the Craft subscribed as a whole. In the lodge, all men were equal; lodge officers were elected by the members and their period of tenure of office was limited. These ideas, in the days of absolute monarchies, were subversive, and even in Britain where there was some degree of representative government they could be regarded as potentially dangerous.

THE ROAD TO WAR

In 1759 measures were introduced in the American colonies to enhance the power of British Customs officials that were regarded as the precursors of tax increases, which, indeed, they soon proved to be. In 1765 came the Stamp Act which

led to the cry of "No taxation without representation."
A new movement emerged in New York that called itself "The Sons of Liberty," an example to be followed in several more of the colonies. The Stamp Act was soon repealed, but it was quickly followed by a series of new Customs duties that proved difficult to collect because of the activities of the Sons of Liberty. Eventually the whole issue focused on a tax on tea, a most unpopular measure that led to the celebrated Boston Tea Party. A ship loaded with tea docked in Boston in

September 1773 and was prevented from unloading by the Sons of Liberty. If the vessel was not unloaded within 20 days, the owners would forfeit the cargo in lieu of Customs duty—and the port officials refused permission for the ship to sail without first being unloaded.

The lodge minutes of the St. Andrew Lodge, which met at Boston's Freemasons' Hall, record that on the night of December 16, 1773 "the lodge was closed until tomorrow evening." There was good reason for this entry, for many of the lodge members were otherwise engaged. Freemasons

"LODGE CLOSED UNTIL TOMORROW"

ON THE NIGHT OF DECEMBER 16, 1773 THE MINUTES OF ST. ANDREW LODGE, BOSTON, REVEAL THAT "THE LODGE IS CLOSED UNTIL TOMORROW EVENING." LODGE MEMBERS JOHN HANCOCK, JOSEPH WARREN, PAUL REVERE, AND EDWARD PROCTOR, ALONG WITH 60 COMPANIONS, WERE BUSY THROWING A CARGO OF TEA INTO THE HARBOR—AN EVENT KNOWN AS THE "BOSTON TEA PARTY."

BELOW: THE BOSTON TEA PARTY,
THE INCIDENT THAT PROVOKED
REBELLION WHEN MEMBERS OF THE
ST. ANDREW LODGE AND OTHER
BOSTONIANS THREW A CARGO OF
TEA INTO BOSTON HARBOR RATHER
THAN PAY THE DUTY ON IT.

RIGHT: GEORGE WASHINGTON,
IN FULL MASONIC REGALIA,
PARTICIPATING AT A FORMAL
LODGE MEETING.

from St. Andrew Lodge, including John Hancock, Joseph
Warren, and Paul Revere, joined with another mason from
the same lodge, Edward Proctor, who was captain of the
militia supposedly guarding the ship, and, in company with
many others, 60 in all, disguised themselves as Native
Americans, boarded the ship and tossed 340 chests of tea
into Boston Harbor. It is recorded that a further 12 men
from this raiding party later joined St. Andrew Lodge.

When civil strife first began, letters and delegates were
sent from Boston asking that Bonnie Prince Charlie consider

becoming King of the Americans, an invitation that was
considered but ultimately rejected by the Stuart heir. As
outright war began, the colonists were divided: many
stayed loyal to the British Crown, while others joined the
fight for freedom. The rebellious colonists fought with
consummate skill and commendable courage, whereas
the British army, for all its experience, behaved with
considerable ineptitude. The American War of
Independence was undoubtedly a war that was fought by
a representative cross-section of colonists, but it was
nonetheless one that had strong Masonic overtones in its
planning and execution. The Boston Tea Party was devised
and executed by Freemasons; they also exerted
considerable influence within the Continental Congress.
The Congressional Committee of Secret Correspondence
was operated by Freemasons. George Washington, the
Commander-in-Chief of the American forces, was a
Freemason, as were many of his generals and a large
number of the men they commanded. Freemasons played
a valiant and influential role in the whole affair, and the
resulting federation of States was clearly founded on

Masonic principles. Yet to describe it as a war instigated or fought by Freemasonry is completely wrong. Freemasons, as individuals, played a valiant part on both sides of the conflict, and although Masonic ideals undoubtedly inspired the country that was being founded, Freemasonry as an organization took no part in this war at all.

STATEHOOD

Within a relatively short time after the end of the War of Independence new Grand Lodges formed in the United States and American Freemasons thus were able to secede from the control previously exercised by the Grand Lodge in London. Many anti-Masonic critics who have studied membership of the Craft have pointed out that in America and in Europe Masonic membership can often be perceived to be a prerequisite to high political office. Because Freemasonry has usually drawn its members from every class in society, it has within its ranks a large number of people drawn from the aristocracy, and the professional and the educated classes. It is therefore not surprising that in the historical context it has included a large number of potential and actual politicians and heads of state among its members. From the time of George Washington to that of Gerald R. Ford, it has been claimed that no less than 14 presidents of the United States have been Freemasons. The Declaration of Independence was signed by nine members of the Craft, and after the end of the War of Independence, Masonic thinking exerted a profound influence on the document that is now regarded as the embodiment of the highest ideals of democracy, the Constitution of the United States.

This important document, which laid the foundations for American democracy, was drafted by the Constitutional Convention which met in Philadelphia, Pennsylvania, between May 25 and September 17, 1787. It is now the oldest written constitution of any state that is still in effect today, and has, right at its heart, the democratic concept that all forms of government must be confined by the rule of law. In many ways the embodiment of the principles of the eighteenth century Age of Enlightenment, it was deeply influenced not only by Masonic belief but also by a variety of philosophers including John Locke, Voltaire, Montesquieu,

and Thomas Paine—men who had all attacked despotic government and suggested that democratic power should arise from below and not be imposed from above. The Declaration of Arbroath held that the King of the Scots derived his sole basis of power from the consent of his people. It was a principle that was fundamental to Masonic thinking. Now, the American Constitution proclaimed that its government could derive its powers only from the consent of the governed, and that all free men have certain natural

and inalienable rights that must be respected by any form of governance. Central to this was the basic Masonic concept that men are born equal and should be treated as equal before the law.

THE SIGNING OF THE AMERICAN CONSTITUTION, THE OLDEST WRITTEN CONSTITUTION STILL IN EFFECT TODAY, ONE THAT ENSHRINES MASONIC IDEALS THAT ALL MEN ARE BORN EQUAL AND THAT A GOVERNMENT CAN ONLY RULE WITH THE CONSENT OF ITS PEOPLE.

THE AMERICAN CONSTITUTION

The Articles of Confederation, which resulted from the colonists' innate hostility to British rule, were founded upon the colonists' revulsion against any form of strong national authority and were framed in such a way that virtually all effective power was left in local hands. The constitution of the United States of America worked on the reasonable assumption that it was not merely wise but practicable to distribute and balance powers between different arms of

government, giving defined local powers and a large degree of autonomy to state governments, and general powers to the national government. This was done in a manner which made it clear that all residual powers remained with the state governments. The extensive powers of the president were prescribed by clearly designated responsibilities, and Montesquieu's concept of the separation and balance of power was adopted with enthusiasm. John Adams proclaimed that the eight explicit balancing mechanisms

within the Constitution were shining examples of the document's republican virtue.

The basic principles of democracy and equality were enshrined right at the beginning of the constitution with the immortal resounding phrase "We the People." However, despite the concept that "all men are born equal and

FIRST PUBLIC READING OF THE AMERICAN DECLARATION OF INDEPENDENCE, IN PHILADELPHIA.

ADOPTED ON JULY 4, 1776, THIS IMAGE APPEARED IN *HARPER'S WEEKLY* IN 1880.

entitled to equal treatment before the law," there were two groups of people who were rigorously and ruthlessly excluded from the protection of the new constitution: the slave population of the Southern states and the Native Americans. Eventually, these fundamentally unjust omissions were corrected, although that took nearly two centuries to complete. The American Constitution certainly contained a number of human imperfections but was framed with such wisdom that it has proved capable of further amendment and development and has evolved into the superb guarantee of people's rights to be governed under the law that obtains today. In the limitations it imposes on central power and the autonomy that it grants to State governments under that central authority, it tends to reflect the situation that obtains in the relations between various Masonic Lodges and the Grand Lodge that supervises them. In Freemasonry, both Officers at Lodge and Grand Lodge levels are elected by secret ballot for strictly defined periods of time. This is replicated under the American Constitution and all those that are modeled upon it, to the extent that we now take these issues for granted. However, at the time it was written, the Constitution of the United States had only one template to consult which embodied these principles: the Constitutions of Freemasonry.

THE DECLARATION OF THE RIGHTS OF MAN

The Constitution of the United States was not the only ringing endorsement of Masonic idealism that became an integral part of humankind's march toward democracy, freedom, and equality. When the Marquis de Lafayette returned to France, he had not merely gained experience in the art of war but was a Freemason of repute who was imbued with democratic principles enshrined

1880

MECHANISMS OF CONSTITUTION
THE STATES VERSUS THE CENTRAL GOVERNMENT
THE HOUSE OF REPRESENTATIVES VERSUS THE SENATE
THE PRESIDENT VERSUS CONGRESS
THE COURTS VERSUS CONGRESS
THE SENATE VERSUS THE PRESIDENT (IN RESPECT OF APPOINTMENTS AND TREATIES)
THE PEOPLE VERSUS THEIR REPRESENTATIVES
THE STATE LEGISLATURES VERSUS THE SENATE (IN THE ORIGINAL ELECTION OF SENATORS)
THE ELECTORAL COLLEGE VERSUS THE PEOPLE

in the American Declaration of Independence. It was Lafayette who first drafted the "Declaration of the Rights of Man" and proposed to the new constituent assembly in France that it be adopted as the opening to the new Constitution that was then being discussed. This new declaration was a considerably expanded version of its American prototype and consisted of a preamble and 17 articles which proclaimed and defined the concepts of political equality and liberty in their various manifestations. It was adopted by the Assembly and accepted by the King on October 5, 1789.

The intellectual fervor that long preceded the French Revolution had been heightened by the activities of a branch of the Invisible College known as the Correspondence Societies who, along with Freemasons and other philosophers and free-thinkers, had helped bring to birth and to public notice the Masonic and egalitarian concepts of *liberté*, *egalité*, and *fraternité* that not only inspired the Revolution but swept right around the world inspiring all the oppressed to seek Freedom, Equality, and Brotherhood. However, it must be remembered that, as with the recent War of Independence in the United States, whereas many Freemasons were active in revolutionary movements, others, often from the same lodges, were at the same time heavily engaged in supporting conservative right-wing monarchist political causes. Freemasons who were active in the French Revolution were actually rather few, and included Georges Danton, Camille Desmoulins, and the Abbé Sieyès. However, the majority of French Freemasons at that time were also members of the bourgeoisie or of the aristocracy, and, in the ensuing Terror, like some of their more revolutionary counterparts, they were led to the guillotine. Indeed, many French Freemasons during the Revolution had somewhat divided loyalties. The Marquis de Lafayette stood back from the violence and took no part in the struggle, for he was not enamoured of civil war in which Frenchman fought Frenchman. Later, he described the Revolution as having no beginning and no end: it was merely part of the on-going campaign for the victory of what is right over inherited privilege.

After the revolution, a right-wing priest, the Abbé Barruel, wrote a book called *Mémoires pour servir à l'histoire du jacobinisme*, which is a mine of anti-Masonic misinformation that "proved," to the Abbé's satisfaction at least, that the entire French Revolution was simply the bloody aftermath of a plot instigated to overthrow both royal and Church authority. This distorted and venomous work was one of the first to give voice to vehement anti-Masonic propaganda and has ultimately led to the modern fantasy of a conspiracy by Freemasons and Jews who wish to create a revolution that will usher in a "New World Order." The initial response at the time was a further wave of anti-Masonic activity involving various hysterical denunciations of the Craft, which caused Freemasonry to be banned in Russia from 1797 to 1803 and later to be ruthlessly suppressed in that country in 1826. In various parts of Europe, unceasing opposition from the Catholic Church stimulated many within European Freemasonry to adopt an anti-clerical attitude that persists in some quarters to this day. It was an attitude that was to bring little comfort or peace of mind to either Freemasonry or the Church.

THE LAST KING OF FRANCE, LOUIS XVI, MOUNTS THE SCAFFOLD FOR HIS EXECUTION BY GUILLOTINE ON JANUARY 21, 1793.

eighteenth-century developments in europe

DISSENT AND DIVISION AMONG FREEMASONS SPREADS THROUGHOUT EUROPE AS A RESULT OF THE SECULARIZATION OF THE CRAFT BY THE GRAND ORIENT OF FRANCE.

PASTEL PAINTING OF A MASON IN THE TEMPLAR REGALIA OF THE ROYAL ARCH, PICTURED AT ROSSLYN CHAPEL.

In the turbulent years that followed the French Revolution, Freemasonry in France suffered a severe decline in membership and cohesion. Indeed, at one time it almost ceased to exist. The French Grand Orient, the governing body, did not re-establish itself until 1795, and a short time later it was followed by another, but smaller, Grand Lodge. The two combined in 1799 and were later joined by a variety of lodges of the Scottish Rite. Some of the latter preferred independence, and in 1804 founded their own governing organization called the Supreme Council of the Ancient and Accepted Scottish Rite. In the confusion that seemed endemic in French Freemasonry during the nineteenth century, new rites appeared with bewildering speed, and a variety of "Grand Lodges" of one form or another rose and fell equally

THE GRAND ORIENT OF FRANCE

THE GRAND LODGE OF THE GRAND ORIENT OF FRANCE CHANGED ITS
CONSTITUTION ON 1877 BY REMOVING ALL REFERENCE TO GOD OR A
SUPREME CREATOR. THIS WAS DIAMETRICALLY OPPOSITE TO
FREEMASONRY'S BELIEF THAT A MASON MUST BELIEVE IN A SUPREME
DEITY. THE UNITED GRAND LODGE OF ENGLAND AND THE GREAT
MAJORITY OF OTHER GRAND LODGES IMMEDIATELY WITHDREW
RECOGNITION FROM THE GRAND ORIENT OF FRANCE.

swiftly. It is far from clear whether or not Napoleon was a Freemason; while there is a strong tradition that he was, records offering proof are non-existent. What is demonstrable is that many of his marshals were indeed members of the Craft and proof of this is readily apparent to any visitor to the Masonic Museum maintained at the headquarters of the Grand Orient of France.

The Grand Orient of France was instrumental in assisting Freemasonry to implant itself firmly in many other European countries, where Grand Lodges were soon founded, named after and modeled upon the Grand Orient. However, the Grand Orient of France chose to express its anti-clerical stance in 1877 by changing its constitution in a manner which removed all reference to God or a Supreme Creator. It substituted the clause: "Freemasonry's basis is in the absolute liberty of conscience and the solidarity of Humanity." All mention of God was expunged from the Craft rituals so that no one could be excluded on account of his beliefs. This act was in direct violation of what all other Freemasons regarded as the first and most important benchmark of the fraternity: namely that a mason must have a belief in a Supreme Deity, who is described within the Craft as the "Great Architect of the Universe." The United Grand Lodge of England and the vast majority of North American Grand Lodges immediately severed all relations with the Grand Orient of France, and withdrew recognition and visiting rights from all lodges under the control of the Grand Orient on the basis that they could not recognize as "true and genuine brethren" anyone who had been initiated in lodges which either deny or ignore that fundamental belief in a Supreme Creator. As far as the United Grand

Lodge of England and its allies were concerned, regular Masonry disappeared from France in 1877 and did not re-appear until 1913.

One result that flowed from the Grand Orient of France's removal of the benchmark of belief in a supreme Deity and the hostility shown to the Church by Italian Freemasons was the issuing of a papal encyclical which accused Freemasons of "following the Evil One." Pope Leo XIII issued this damning indictment of the Craft, *Humanum Genus*, in 1884, in which he stated categorically that Freemasonry has as its aim "overthrowing all the religious and social orders introduced by Christianity, and building a new one according to its taste, based on the foundation and laws of naturalism." The Pope warned the world that the Masonic aims of promoting democracy and secular education would lead to "universal revolution and subversion." Leo begged civil rulers to unite with the Church and "root out this poison," and ended his letter by imploring the Virgin Mary to "aid the Church against ... impious sects in which one sees the ... shrewdness of Satan."

THE REUNIFICATION OF ITALY

The creation of a united kingdom within Italy had been a long-held dream among the Rex Deus families of the northern Italian states for centuries—indeed, ever since the last Visconti dukes had ruled Milan. It fell to two Freemasons to bring this dream to reality in the later part of the nineteenth century. They played a major role in the campaign for the reunification of Italy through their influence on the secret society known as the Carbonari, who were the prime movers in the struggle to unite this country under one monarch, to free many of its states from rule by foreign nations, and to remove the malign hand of the Pope and the Inquisition from their positions of absolute power in the Papal States. Both of the principal leaders of this revolutionary movement, Garibaldi and Mazzini, were Freemasons, and in 1870 their armies liberated Rome from the tyranny of the papacy and gave a vibrant reality to the old Visconti dream of a united kingdom of Italy. Pope Pius IX was stripped of all temporal power, and the specter of the Inquisition began to fade from the Italian consciousness. The

LEFT: A MASONIC LODGE SEAL, DATING FROM THE END OF THE EIGHTEENTH CENTURY.

BELOW: A MEETING OF THE GRAND ORIENT OF FRANCE, DATE UNKNOWN.

Pope began a lifelong exile in his self-imposed prison, the tiny and autonomous city-state of the Vatican.

Pius IX believed he knew only too well who were the true authors of his debasement, and he fulminated furiously against the Freemasons in a series of encyclicals, papal bulls, and allocutions. Unlike many Masonic historians today, the Pope had few illusions as to the true origins of the "diabolical organization" that had stripped him of earthly power. In his eyes, Freemasonry was the undoubted heir to the heretical Order of the Knights Templar whom he described as being followers of the Johannine heresy and Gnostic from the very start. And how could he be in error? After all, he was the pope who had promulgated the dogma of Papal Infallibility.

It would be misleading to describe Freemasons who engaged in the politics of that or any other era as being dedicated to revolution. Any list of nineteenth-century politically active members of the Craft is remarkably inconsistent when viewed in political terms, for it includes, on the progressive and revolutionary side, the men who worked for social change and extended democratic principles—men such as Mazzini and Garibaldi in Italy, Daniel O'Connell and Henry Grattan in Ireland, and Bakunin and Kerensky in Russia—and on the other hand it includes politically active Masons of a very different hue: three French Presidents, two kings of Prussia (who could hardly be described as democratic), the arch-turncoat Talleyrand, various kings of Great Britain, the right-wing administrator and poet Goethe, to say nothing of the vast swathe of English aristocrats with a strong leavening of Anglican clergy who formed the backbone of the political establishment in

the United Kingdom. Similarly, in South America, although many of the leaders of the various liberation movements were indeed Freemasons of note, so too were many of the people they fought against, for a good number of Spanish Viceroys and landowners were also members of the Craft. In Texas at the famous siege of the Alamo, the Texan leaders were all reputedly members of the Freemasons, but so was General Santa Anna, their opponent. These acute differences of perspective that were found in the political life of many

Freemasons were replicated within the Craft to a certain extent, and produced some of the differences, schisms and splits mentioned earlier. For a fraternity dedicated to brotherhood and unity, there was, in truth, a tendency toward a growing lack of mutual recognition, amity and visiting rights between the various jurisdictions that came into existence under a plethora of Grand Lodges.

One Grand Lodge above all others took signal steps to bring order out of this emerging chaos, and, at the same

time, instilled a far greater degree of religious freedom into a fraternity that was already extremely tolerant.

THE UNITED GRAND LODGE OF ENGLAND

The United Grand Lodge of England has often been criticized for its dismissive attitude toward the history of the origins of the Craft, but few can fault it for the stand it has taken, since its inception, toward creating order out of the chaos to which the worldwide Craft was inevitably heading, or toward clarifying and establishing what is, and what is not, true Freemasonry.

Freemasons' Hall in London was the scene of a great celebration on December 27, 1813 as the Premier and Antients Grand Lodges formally joined together to create the United Grand Lodge of England. The Prince of Wales, who had formally been the Grand Master of the Premier Lodge, had since become Prince Regent, and in court circles it had been decided that no monarch or his regent could hold any

BELOW: ROBBIE BURNS BEING INAUGURATED AS THE POET LAUREATE OF THE LODGE, CANNONGATE, KILWINNING, EDINBURGH.

RIGHT: STAMP OF A MASONIC LODGE FROM THE LATE EIGHTEENTH CENTURY, DISPLAYING THE ANCIENT EGYPTIAN SYMBOLISM OF THE PYRAMID ENCLOSING THE ALL-SEEING EYE OF HORUS.

position that was subject to an annual election that he could theoretically lose. The Prince of Wales therefore resigned as Grand Master of the Premier Lodge, and his brother, HRH Augustus Frederick, Duke of Sussex, was elected Grand Master on the April 7, 1813. The Duke of Kent was installed as Grand Master of the Antients Grand Lodge on December 1. At the time of the union of the two Grand Lodges, the Duke of Kent resigned his position and nominated his brother, the Duke of Sussex, as the first Grand Master of the United Grand Lodge of England.

With the wondrous benefit of hindsight it is now obvious that from the point of view of Freemasonry in Britain, if not the world, the Grand Lodge could hardly have chosen a more appropriate Grand Master. The Duke of Sussex was blessed with attributes which were to inspire the Craft to new heights of

development. He was young, well liked, remarkably tolerant for a man of his time, industrious, and absolutely dedicated to Freemasonry. It would appear that the Grand Master had four principal ambitions that, over time, he achieved. Firstly, he meant to establish the United Grand Lodge of England's authority over all the lodges that had previously been subject to direction from the two constituent Grand Lodges which had so recently merged. His other objectives included the standardizing of the three degrees of Craft Masonry and the degrees of the Royal Arch, then the removal from them of all overtly Christian references so as to make them accessible and attractive to men of other faiths. Lastly he wished to maintain the Craft's superiority over all other Masonic Orders. And, to a very large extent, he succeeded.

Standardization began at once. Wisely, the articles of union for the two previous Grand Lodges had laid down the framework necessary for a special "Lodge of Reconciliation" that was charged with the task of reconciling the two earlier patterns of ritual and creating a standardized form that could be adopted by all the lodges in England. The new changes shifted the emphasis within Freemasonry from one of

THE DUKE OF SUSSEX

AS FIRST GRAND MASTER OF THE UNITED GRAND LODGE OF ENGLAND HE ESTABLISHED U.G.L.E.'S AUTHORITY OVER ALL THE LODGES OF ENGLAND, AND STANDARDIZED ALL THE DEGREES OF CRAFTMASONRY AND THE ROYAL ARCH.

LEFT: FREEMASONS' HALL WAS REBUILT IN LONDON'S GREAT QUEEN STREET BETWEEN 1927 AND 1933.

OPPOSITE: MASONIC APRON AND OTHER RITUAL ARTIFACTS. FROM AN EARLY LITHOGRAPHIC PLATE USED IN THE 1895 EDITION OF GOULD'S *HISTORY OF FREEMASONRY*.

conviviality to one wherein ritual instruction focused far more heavily on the spiritual pathway to morality and true fraternity. However, because the ritual had to be learned by word of mouth and could not, at that time, be printed, and although all English lodges began to practice the same basic principles of ritual and formality in their ceremonies, there still remained considerable variation in the wording of these rituals from lodge to lodge. Regalia, however, constituted a different matter. Rules were now created that standardized the designs for Masonic aprons and jewels (as medals are called within the Craft).

Prior to the formation of the United Grand Lodge, English Freemasonry had, like the country in which it arose, been Christian, in that Anglican Christianity was the only formally recognized religion in the land. So it had been natural that Christian references had been incorporated in the earlier rituals. The two St. Johns—John the Baptist and John the Evangelist—were regarded as the patron saints of Freemasonry, as they had once been of the Knights Templar. The ritual installation of lodge officers usually took place on the days dedicated to the two saints: one in June, (St. John the Baptist), and the other in December (St. John the Evangelist). Things had begun to change when Jews were

first admitted in the 1720s. Now, in the early years of the nineteenth century under the benevolent direction of the Duke of Sussex, this change accelerated rapidly. The Duke, a supporter of the move toward Catholic emancipation and a Hebrew scholar of some distinction, held firmly to the belief that Freemasonry was originally intended to be open to all who believed in a Supreme Being. It was for this reason that he enthusiastically encouraged the de-Christianization of the three Craft degrees and then turned his attention to the Royal arch degrees with the same intent.

The new United Grand Lodge was not merely intent on creating a new and enlightened sense of fraternity within the lodges under its own jurisdiction, but right from the very beginning it sought mutual recognition and cooperation with the Grand Lodges of both Ireland and Scotland

Representatives from all three Grand Lodges met in London in 1814 and came to an agreement known as the International Compact. Each Grand Lodge recognized the sovereignty of the others and their sole rights in their own territories. Areas abroad, where no Grand Lodges existed, were regarded as free territories in which any of the three Grand Lodges could warrant lodges under their own jurisdiction. This happy state of affairs has lasted ever since. Indeed, the three Grand Lodges in the British Isles, the lineal descendants of the originators of Freemasonry, are looked upon by all other regular Grand Lodges as the guardians of Masonic regularity. Thus, when new a Grand Lodge is founded elsewhere in the world, it is recognition by the three British Grand Lodges that establishes the "regularity" of the new Grand Lodge. If such recognition is denied, the new Grand Lodge is regarded as "irregular" by all recognized Grand Lodges.

The matter of regularity became a major cause for concern in the mid-1870s when, as noted above, the Grand Orient of France removed all mention of God from its Constitutions and rituals and then proceeded to remove the Bible from its lodges. This was far from the only basis for withdrawing recognition cited by supporters of the United Grand Lodge of England. The Grand Orient of France was accused of becoming too political in its stance—perhaps as a reaction against the wave of rabid anti-Masonry that swept France at that time, and perhaps for other reasons. However, the troubles in French Freemasonry were not over. Another issue arose which has reverberations even today in the twenty-first century: the admission of women into Freemasonry.

Traditionally, as recorded in the Landmarks of Freemasonry, only men can become Masons. However, there was an early exception to this that is a matter of record: a woman was initiated as a Mason—a young lady named Elizabeth St. Leger, the daughter of the first Viscount Doneraile of County Cork in Ireland. Her father held lodge meetings in his house, and one day Elizabeth was discovered watching a meeting through a small hole in the wall. This caused a great degree of consternation in the Lodge, and, after prolonged discussion, the members decided that the young woman should be initiated into the fraternity. She later became a subscriber to the Irish Book of Constitutions of 1744, and it is recorded that she attended Masonic events wearing her regalia. At her death she was accorded a full Masonic funeral. But this episode was an aberration, and the bar against women remained inviolable until the late nineteenth century.

A lady called Maria Deraismes was initiated into Freemasonry at the Loge Libre Penseurs in France on January 14, 1882. This had previously been a male lodge that fell under the jurisdiction of the Grand Loge Symbolique de France, which had seceded from the Grand Orient in 1879. Loge Libre Penseurs was immediately suspended for the impropriety of admitting a woman into the Craft. One of the members of Libre Penseurs was Dr. Georges Martin, who was a member of the French Senate and an advocate of women's rights. He was also a member of another lodge,

La Jérusalem Écossaisse, and there he proposed the creation of an Order that would admit women to its ranks. On March 14, Dr. Martin and several other male Masons founded La Respectable Loge, Le Droit Humain Macconerie Mixte, the Worshipful Lodge, Human Rights, Co-Masonry, in Paris, which initiated, passed, and raised 16 candidates who were all female. In 1893 on April 4, a Grand Lodge was established called La Grande Loge Symbolique Écossaise de France, Le Droit Humain, The Scottish Symbolic Grand

Lodge, Human Rights. This signaled a dramatic change in an otherwise all-male fraternity and opened parts of it up to members of both sexes. Since then the arguments have raged unceasingly but—strangely—the United Grand Lodge of England, while cleaving as ever to the old traditions of the Craft and refusing to recognize co-masonry as regular, does admit that women may nonetheless be regarded as part of Freemasonry when describing Freemasonry in general.

THE INITIATION OF A WOMAN IN ONE OF THE FRENCH JURISDICTIONS DURING THE LATE NINETEENTH CENTURY.

glimpses from within

AS IT HAS EVOLVED, THE DEBATE WITHIN THE CRAFT'S RANKS AS TO WHAT DOES, OR DOES NOT, CONSTITUTE TRUE FREEMASONRY HAS DEEPENED AND HAS ULTIMATELY BEEN DEFINED BY THE UNITED GRAND LODGE OF ENGLAND.

F ounded many centuries ago on the three great principles of brotherly love, relief, and truth, Freemasonry aims to bring together men of goodwill, regardless of background and opinion. The society began to define its responsibilities and obligations shortly after the foundation of the First Grand Lodge in London. In 1720, the Grand Master compiled the "general regulations," which, after approval by the Grand Lodge, were published in 1723. One of these regulations reads as follows:

Every Annual Grand Lodge has an inherent power and Authority to make new Regulations or to alter these, for the real benefits of this Ancient Fraternity; provided always that the old Land-Marks be carefully preserved.

These Landmarks, which were eventually to define the essential character of Freemasonry, were not defined at the time. Indeed, it would appear that they were held to be self-evident and were simply believed to be "those peculiar marks by which we are able to designate our inheritance."

Over the centuries, there has been a continuous dispute to define what are and are not the true Masonic landmarks. Some authorities restrict them to the obligation signs, tokens, and words that are secret in the fraternity. Others include ceremonies of initiation, the ornaments, furniture, and jewels of a lodge, and the characteristic symbols. All of these, because they are loose and unsatisfactory, have been subject to ongoing debate. Perhaps the safest approach is the one that restricts them to those ancient and therefore universal customs of the Order that have existed for so long that no account of their origin exists.

THE DEBATE BEGINS

Masonic Landmarks were mentioned in George Payne's *General Regulations*, which was published along with James Anderson's *Constitutions* in 1723. Payne was apparently referring to the old traditional secrets relevant to the effective construction of buildings. William Preston, in

AN EARLY NINETEENTH-CENTURY DEPICTION OF A BLINDFOLDED MALE CANDIDATE BEING INITIATED INTO THE FIRST DEGREE— "THE ENTERED APPRENTICE."

Illustrations of Masonry published in 1772, uses the term "Landmarks" as if they were synonymous with established usages and customs of the Masonic Craft, and claims that the ritual of the Master Mason's Degree preserves them; and his hypothesis was expressly sanctioned by the Grand Lodge of England at that time. Furthermore, he cites the charges used in the installation of the master elect, wherein that officer is required to promise to "strictly conform to every edict of the Grand Lodge which is not subversive to the principles of Masonry," adding the stricture "that it is not within the power of any man or body of men to make alterations or innovations in the body of Masonry." Yet what the landmarks actually were was still not clarified.

A formal attempt to define them was made by Albert Mackey in 1858 when he published *The Foundation of Masonic Law* in a Masonic journal. Mackey defined landmarks as "those ancient and universal customs of the Order, which either gradually grew into operation as rules of action, or, if at once enacted by any competent authority, were enacted at a period so remote that no account of their origin is to be found in the record of history." He also defined the three requisite characteristics of landmarks that are still generally accepted today. These are: (a) immemorial antiquity; (b) universality; and (c) absolute irrevocability. He then proceeded to list 25 landmarks that were later published in a volume entitled the *Text Book of Masonic Jurisprudence*. These landmarks were generally accepted by many American Freemasons of that time, and, indeed, were adopted by some North American Grand Lodges. However, today Albert Mackey's landmarks of Freemasonry are, more often than not, hotly disputed.

In 1863, George Oliver published his *Freemason's Treasury,* which listed 40 landmarks. So the situation in this apparently basic issue was, to say the least, confused, and still remains so. For example, over the last century or more a number of American Grand Lodges have attempted the daunting task of enumerating the landmarks, coming to widely varying conclusions. West Virginia established seven, New Jersey ten, Nevada 39, and Kentucky 54. H. B. Grant also listed 54 landmarks in the *Masonic Home Journal* of 1889, and this particular list has been frequently reprinted.

DEPICTION OF THE FINAL PART OF
THE THIRD DEGREE, THE RAISING
OF A MASTER MASON. THE LIT
CANDLES SYMBOLIZE HIS PASSAGE
FROM DEATH INTO THE LIGHT
OF SPIRITUAL ENLIGHTENMENT.
THE ILLUSTRATION SHOWS
EIGHTEENTH-CENTURY MASONS.

SIMPLIFYING THE LANDMARKS

In 1918, the Grand Lodge of Massachusetts adopted
a considerably shortened list, namely:

- Monotheism, the sole dogma of Freemasonry
- Belief in immortality, the ultimate lesson of Masonic
  philosophy
- The Volume of Sacred Law, an indispensable part
  of the furniture of the lodge
- The legend of the Third Degree
- Secrecy
- The Symbolism of the Operative Art
- A Mason must be a free-born adult.

However, the lodge added a rider that this list was not to be
deemed exclusive. Roscoe Pound, one-time Professor of Law
at Harvard and a Past Master of the Craft, wrote in his book
Masonic Jurisprudence in 1941 that: "these principles, this
groundwork, this body of Masonry, whether we use the
term 'landmarks' or not, convey the very idea which has
become familiar to us by that name." He then reduced the
list to the six landmarks that he believed were essential:

- Belief in a Supreme Being
- Belief in a persistence of personality
- A book of law as an indispensable part of the
  "furnishings" of the lodge
- The Hiramic legend of the Third Degree
- The symbolism of the operative art
- That a Mason be a man, freeborn, and of age.

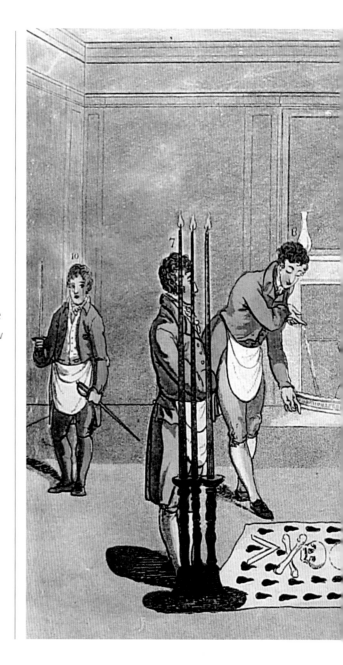

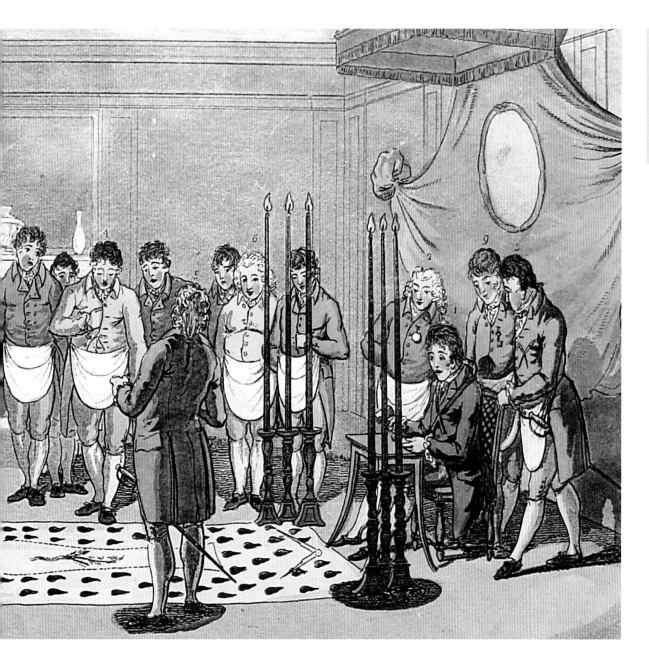

The belief in a Supreme Being, generally described as The Great Architect of the Universe, is included in all lists of Masonic landmarks. The second—persistence of personality, or for some Masons, the immortality of the soul—is acceptable by all religions, for even the Buddhist doctrine of the transmigration of souls meets this requirement. The third of Pound's landmarks is "the book of the law, that volume which, by the religion of a country, is believed to contain the revealed word of the Great Architect," which again has a universal application. For Christians it is the Bible, consisting of the Old and New Testaments. For Jews it is the Tanakh, or the Old Testament. For Muslims it is the Holy Koran, and for members of the Hindu faith it is the Shruti. In India during British rule Christians often sat in Lodge with Hindus, Buddists, and Muslims, and these lodges kept a Bible, a Koran, and the Hindu texts on the altar.

The fourth landmark is one of the few enunciated by Mackey that is widely accepted. Indeed, he said of the Hiramic legend of the Third Degree that "any rite that excluded it or materially altered it would at once cease to be a Masonic rite." The fifth landmark is symbolism which, within Masonry, is deemed to be immemorial and universal, having been inherited from the early rites of the medieval Craftmasons. The sixth supports the age-old tradition that a Mason must be a freeborn man, of full age by law, according to the custom of the place, and harks back to the medieval days when one was either "free-born"—i.e. a noble, knight, or skilled craftsman—or one tied to the land and his lord, such as a bondsman, a serf, a laborer, or an unskilled person.

Today, the majority of Masonic scholars agree on two essential points that a true landmark must fulfill in order to gain universal acceptance: it must have existed from the "time whereof the memory of man runneth not to the contrary" and be of such fundamental and universal importance that Freemasonry would no longer be Freemasonry if it were removed. Perhaps one of the best summations of the landmarks was devised when the Grand Lodge of British Columbia adopted the following passage in lieu of the first paragraph in Anderson:

STANDARDS TO BE MET BY A JURISDICTION SEEKING RECOGNITION BY THE UNITED GRAND LODGE OF ENGLAND

IT MUST HAVE BEEN LAWFULLY ESTABLISHED BY A "REGULAR" GRAND LODGE OR BY THREE OR MORE PRIVATE LODGES, EACH WARRANTED BY A REGULAR GRAND LODGE.

IT MUST BE TRULY INDEPENDENT AND SELF-GOVERNING, WITH UNDISPUTED AUTHORITY OVER CRAFT FREEMASONRY (I.E. THE THREE SYMBOLIC DEGREES OF ENTERED APPRENTICE, FELLOW CRAFT AND MASTER MASON) WITHIN ITS JURISDICTION AND NOT SUBJECT IN ANY WAY TO, OR SHARING POWER WITH, ANY OTHER MASONIC BODY.

FREEMASONS UNDER ITS JURISDICTION MUST BE MEN, AND ITS LODGES MUST HAVE NO MASONIC CONTACT WITH LODGES WHICH ADMIT WOMEN TO MEMBERSHIP.

FREEMASONS UNDER ITS JURISDICTION MUST BELIEVE IN A SUPREME BEING.

ALL FREEMASONS UNDER ITS JURISDICTION MUST TAKE THEIR OBLIGATIONS ON, OR IN FULL VIEW OF, THE VOLUME OF SACRED LAW (I.E. THE BIBLE, OR THE BOOK HELD SACRED BY THE MAN CONCERNED).

THE THREE GREAT LIGHTS OF FREEMASONRY (I.E. THE VOLUME OF SACRED LAW, THE SQUARE, AND THE COMPASSES) MUST BE ON DISPLAY WHEN THE GRAND LODGE OR ITS SUBORDINATE LODGES ARE OPEN.

THE DISCUSSION OF RELIGION AND POLITICS WITHIN ITS LODGES MUST BE PROHIBITED.

IT MUST ADHERE TO THE ESTABLISHED PRINCIPLES AND TENETS (THE "ANCIENT LANDMARKS") AND CUSTOMS OF THE CRAFT, AND INSIST ON THEIR BEING OBSERVED WITHIN ITS LODGES.

A Freemason is obliged, by his tenure, to obey the moral law; and if he rightly understands the Art he will never be an atheist nor an irreligious libertine. He, of all men, should best understand that God seeth not as man seeth; for man looketh at the outward appearance, but God looketh to the heart. A Freemason is, therefore,

ABOVE: A MASONIC MEDALLION OR JEWEL DISPLAYING MASONIC AND HERMETIC SYMBOLISM, INCLUDING THE TOOLS OF THE CRAFT AND REFERENCES TO ITS EGYPTIAN ORIGINS.

LEFT: A TYPICAL TEACHING, OR TRACING, BOARD DISPLAYING MUCH OF THE SYMBOLISM USED IN MASONIC RITUAL: THE THREE PILLARS THAT SUPPORT A TRUE LODGE, THE RITUAL BLACK AND WHITE CARPET, OR CHECKERBOARD OF JOY, MASONIC TOOLS USED TO PREPARE THE STONE, AND THE ASCENT TOWARD THE LIGHT.

A TYPICAL THIRD DEGREE
TRACING BOARD SHOWING
THE SYMBOLISM OF THE
CHECKERBOARD OF JOY,
THE MEMENTO MORI OF THE
SKULL AND CROSS BONES,
THE TOOLS OF CRAFTMASONRY,
AND THE ACACIA TREE.

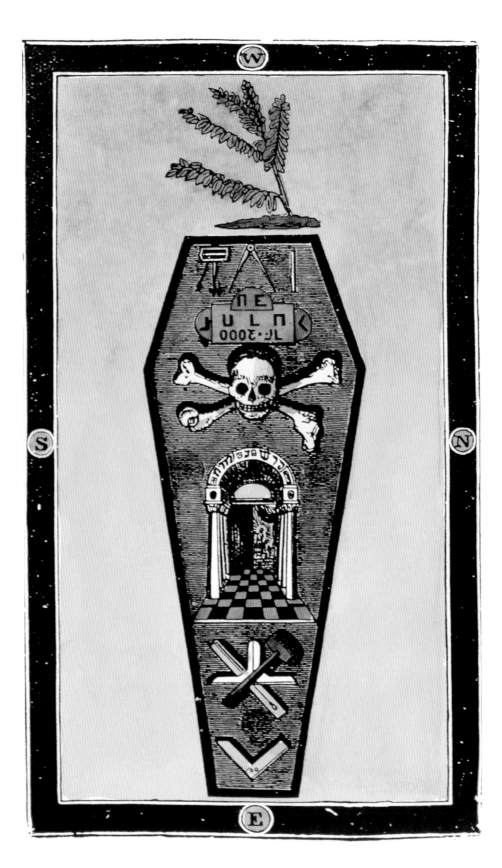

particularly bound never to act against the dictates of his conscience. Let a man's religion or mode of worship be what it may, he is not excluded from the Order, provided he believe in the glorious Architect of heaven and earth, and practise the sacred duties of morality. Freemasons unite with the virtuous of every persuasion in the firm and pleasing bond of fraternal love; they are taught to view the errors of mankind with compassion and to strive, by the purity of their own conduct, to demonstrate the superior excellence of the faith they may profess.

However, for those who believe in clarity and simplicity, one of the most beautiful and comprehensive statements of the landmarks of Freemasonry was written by Joseph Fort Newton, in *The Builder*, when he summarized the landmarks in the following terms: "The fatherhood of God, the brotherhood of man, the moral law, the Golden Rule, and the hope of life everlasting."

THE PROMISES MADE BY FREEMASONS

All new members seeking admission to the Craft are required to make certain solemn promises with regard to their behavior not merely in the Lodge but also within society as a whole. The promises resemble the familiar oaths that are taken in courts of law or on admission to the armed services and many other organizations. The only difference is that candidate swears to keep confidential all the signs and passwords that identify him as a Mason when seeking entry into a lodge where he is not known. The rather savage and bloodthirsty "traditional penalties" that used to be so beloved of the anti-Masonic fraternity were dropped some decades ago, and furthermore were always symbolic and never literal. They were an allegory for the way any man of honor would feel emotionally at the thought of violating his word. Members also undertake never to make use of their membership of the Craft of Freemasonry for personal gain or advancement. Failure to observe this principle or falling below the expected standards of Freemasonry in any other significant way can result in expulsion from the Craft on a charge of "un-Masonic conduct."

THE ROLE OF GRAND LODGES

Freemasonry is regulated by a variety of Grand Lodges, most of which support principles and standards that were originally set by the Grand Lodge of England and that have been maintained by the United Grand Lodge of England throughout its history. For a Grand Lodge Jurisdiction to be recognized by the United Grand Lodge of England, it must meet certain standards (*see box on page 110*).

Needless to say, sometimes for the reasons given in the previous chapter, not all Grand Lodges meet these demanding but essential standards.

THE THREE DEGREES OF CRAFT, OR BLUE-LODGE, FREEMASONRY

The prospective candidate for Freemasonry is always interviewed by lodge officers, usually pastmasters, and asked if he believes in God. If the answer is yes and he is proven to be of good character, his name is put before the lodge for election. A secret ballot is held on the candidature, and if passed, the prospective new member is invited to the lodge for initiation into the First Degree, that of "The Entered Apprentice." Blindfolded and shod in slippers, divested of all metallic objects, his left leg exposed to the knee and shirt wide open so that the left breast is bare and with a cable-tow noose around his neck, the candidate is led to the lodge door. There a guard bangs on the door with the hilt of a sword and asks permission for the candidate's entry. With the point of a sword pressing against his exposed breast, the candidate is asked several simple questions with the required answers being prompted by his escort. Among the questions put by the Worshipful Master of the Lodge is this:

THE THREE DEGREES OF FREEMASONRY

⊖ THE FIRST DEGREE: THE ENTERED APPRENTICE
⊖ THE SECOND DEGREE: THE FELLOW CRAFT MASON
⊖ THE THIRD AND FINAL DEGREE:
THE SUBLIME DEGREE OF MASTER MASON

As no man can be made a Mason unless he be free and of a mature age, I now demand of you—are you a free man and of the full age of twenty-one years?

The reply is "Yes."

The Worshipful Master then enquires, in a ritual manner, if the candidate's desire to join Freemasonry is uninfluenced by any mercenary or unworthy motive and is inspired by a favorable opinion of the Order and a desire to render service to his fellow man.

The candidate then kneels and a prayer is said invoking the blessing of the Great Architect of the Universe. After three ritual perambulations around the Lodge, the blindfolded candidate is brought before the Worshipful Master, who says: "Having been in a state of darkness, what is the predominant wish of your heart?" to which the reply is "Light." The Worshipful Master then declaims: "Let the blessing be restored!" and the candidate's blindfold is removed. His attention is then drawn to the three symbolic "lights" of Freemasonry: the Volume of Sacred Law (Bible, Old Tanakh, Holy Koran or other as appropriate), the Square, and the Compasses. At that point the candidate has attained the rank of Entered Apprentice, which is the first of the three Degrees of Craft Masonry. The secret signs of recognition, grips, and passwords of that degree are then explained, before the new "Entered Apprentice" is presented with a plain lambskin apron. The symbolic meaning of the apron is explained, and throughout the remainder of the ritual various moral lessons are imparted using the symbolism of stonemasons' tools perfecting the stones used for sacred buildings.

In the course of this degree and afterward the Entered Apprentice learns to answer certain ritual questions, among which are: "What is Freemasonry?", to which the answer is: "A peculiar system of morality, veiled in allegory and illustrated by symbols"; and "What are the three grand principles upon which Freemasonry is founded?", to which the response must be: "Brotherly love, relief, and truth."

Later, when the Entered Apprentice has made sufficient progress in Masonic knowledge and understanding, he enters the temple in company with his brethren, wearing his white lambskin apron as a sign of his humility. The Lodge is opened in the first degree and the test questions are then put to the apprentice. When his answers are deemed satisfactory, the apprentice is once more led from the Temple and prepared for the "passing ceremony." On this occasion, the left leg and right breast are laid bare and the Apprentice is led around the Temple by the deacon and is given new passwords and signs appropriate to the second degree. More allegorical and symbolic instruction is given, and after the completion of the ritual, the new Fellow Craft Mason is instructed to extend his researches into the hidden mysteries of natural science.

The Fellow Craft Mason is again given a series of test questions which he must be able to answer before being raised to the sublime, third, and final degree of Craft Masonry, the sublime degree of Master Mason. He enters the Temple, which—apart from a small candle burning in the east in front of the Worshipful Master—is in total darkness. He is then informed that the ritual of this degree concerns death. After a brief recital of the previous two degrees, there follows a ritual telling and re-enactment of the story of the murder of Hiram Abif, the builder of the Temple of Solomon, in which the candidate for the degree receives a blow on the temple and collapses onto his right knee. The Worshipful Master then lightly strikes the candidate again on the forehead whereupon he is stretched flat on the floor and a funeral shroud is then draped over the prone body. The junior Warden reaches down, takes the candidate's hand and says, "Worshipful Master, this grip proves to slip." Other figures march around the "corpse," and one is instructed to try again, this time with the Fellow Craft grip. This also fails. The Worshipful Master then speaks, saying:

Brother Wardens, you have both failed ... There remains yet a third and peculiar method, known as the Lion's Paw or Eagle's Claw grip, which is given by taking a firm hold of the sinews of the right wrist and raising him on the five points of fellowship, of which, with your assistance, I will now make a trial.

THE MASONIC SWORD. FOR FREEMASONS THE SWORD HAS ALWAYS BEEN AN INSTRUMENT OF JUSTICE AND TRUTH, AND SYMBOLIZES THESE QUALITIES IN MASONIC RITUAL.

The Worshipful Master then grips the candidate by the wrist and pulls him upright, whispering two words in his ear. Then, out loud, so all can hear, he reminds the candidate of the brevity of life and directs his attention to a skull and the symbolic grave from which he has just been raised. As with the previous two degrees, certain words and grips are given to the new Master Mason who has, allegorically at least, been dead to the things of this world and been resurrected to the realities of the world of the spirit with a stark reminder of his own ultimate mortality.

These brief accounts of the rituals of the three degrees of Freemasonry cannot impart anything like the true flavor of the events they describe. Symbolism can be explained, but it needs to be experienced not once but many times. Nothing but active participation in the rituals of Freemasonry can ever do much more than lightly scratch the surface of these ancient and effective rites. Constant repetition, allegorical teaching, and the power of symbolism bring about subtle, cumulative shifts in consciousness that ultimately help individuals to totally transform their behavior. It is in this slow and careful way that true fraternity and high moral standards can be brought to fruition. And brotherhood, irrespective of race, creed, or color, is the ultimate objective.

brotherhood and charity

THE ELIMINATION OF RACIAL PREJUDICE WITHIN THE WORLDWIDE BROTHERHOOD
OF FREEMASONS, AND THE IMMENSE CHARITABLE CONTRIBUTIONS MADE BY THE
CRAFT THROUGHOUT THE WORLD.

acial prejudice began to be eliminated from Freemasonry very early in the history of the Craft. In British India, for example, it was not uncommon for lodges to have members from Christian, Muslim, and Hindu faiths, and racial origin seemed to play no part in admission procedures. Things were a little different in the American colonies, but even here, people of a different color or racial origin became Masons very early on indeed.

PRINCE HALL FREEMASONRY

The acknowledged "father" of Black Masonry in the United States was a man named Prince Hall. Details of his birth have never been clearly established; according to one account he was a freed slave, in another he was described as born free, though whether this was in Barbados or in Boston, Massachusetts, is unclear. The most credible account claims that he was born of an English father, Thomas Prince Hall, and a free colored woman with mixed French ancestry. In 1765 he established himself in Boston working in the leather trade, eventually buying property there and becoming eligible to vote some eight years later. Black Freemasonry in the Americas began when Prince Hall and 14 other free black men were initiated into one of the British army's traveling lodges, Lodge 441, attached to the 38th Regiment of Foot, which was warranted by the Grand Lodge of Ireland.

The new initiates were named as Prince Hall, Cyrus Johnson, Bueston Slinger, Prince Rees, John Canton, Peter Freeman, Benjamin Tiler, Duff Ruform, Thomas Santerson, Prince Rayden, Cato Speain, Boston Smith, Peter Best, Foten Howard, and Richard Titley. They were all initiated by the Master of the Lodge, Sergeant John Batt. When the British army left Boston in 1776, Lodge 441 granted its black brethren a dispensation to meet as African Lodge 1, to march in procession on St. John's Day, to honor their dead

with Masonic funerals, but, strangely, they were forbidden to confer degrees or perform any Masonic "work." Despite these bizarre limitations on their activities, the original brethren were joined by others who had been initiated elsewhere, and they continued to meet in a regular manner. By 1779 there were 33 masons entered on the roll of the lodge. On March 2, 1784, Prince Hall petitioned the Grand Lodge of England for a warrant to regularize African Lodge 1, using the good offices of William Moody, the Worshipful Master of Brotherly Love Lodge 55 in London. The warrant was granted on September 29, 1784 and was delivered on April 29, 1787 by Captain James Scott. Under the authority of this warrant, African Lodge number 459 was instituted on May 6 that year.

Appointed a Provincial Grand Master by HRH the Prince of Wales in 1791, Prince Hall established other African lodges in Philadelphia and in Providence, Rhode Island, in 1797. The African Lodge 459 of Boston thus became the "Mother Lodge" of a growing Prince Hall family. In 1808, representatives of these lodges met in the city of New York to form the African Grand Lodge. Following the foundation of the United Grand Lodge of England in 1813, the African Grand Lodge was stricken from the rolls of its English "parent" in exactly the same manner as all other American Grand Lodges. Thus began a tradition of a separate African-American Masonic jurisdiction that has lasted down to the twenty-first century and maintained continuous growth. The practice of slavery, and the racism and segregation that lasted for a century after its abolition, made it effectively impossible for a man of color to join a "regular" mainstream lodge in the United States of America. So Prince Hall Freemasonry strode out alone and continued to serve the growing Masonic needs and aspirations of the black community in North America.

Today this vital and vibrant jurisdiction of Freemasonry is recognized as "regular" by 38 of the 55 Grand Lodges in the United States and for the many years that have elapsed since the advent of Civil Rights legislation it has become increasingly common to find people of all ethnic backgrounds in the regular lodges of most of the jurisdictions of the country.

A PARADE OF AFRICAN-AMERICAN FREEMASONS OF THE PRINCE HALL JURISDICTION IN NEW ORLEANS IN THE 1950s.

CHARITABLE FREEMASONRY

EARLY FREEMASONRY CREATED THE FIRST CHARITIES THAT WERE
OUTSIDE THE CONTROL OF THE CHURCH. SINCE THEN THE CRAFT HAS
EXPANDED ITS CHARITABLE ACTIVITIES EXPONENTIALLY AND HAS, IN
ALL JURISDICTIONS, SUPPORTED HOSPITALS, RETIREMENT HOMES,
MEDICAL RESEARCH, CHILDREN'S CHARITIES, AND SCHOOLS, AS WELL
AS CREATING EDUCATIONAL TRUSTS OFFERING SCHOLARSHIPS AND
BURSARIES.

RELIEF OR CHARITY

When Freemasonry first appeared in Scotland it created the
benevolent societies which were the first charitable
institutions in Europe outside the direct control of the
Church. From that time onward, most lodges in Scotland had
benefit societies attached to them. However, in 1846 the
Grand Lodge of Scotland established a body known as the
Grand Lodge Charity Fund to administer relief among the
membership. Another body, the Annuity Fund, was
established in 1888 to take care of the widows and elderly
members. A more specific organization, the Orphan Annuity
Fund, was founded in 1917, and in 1957 the Grand Lodge of
Scotland began purchasing a number of buildings that now
act as old people's homes.

When the Grand Lodge was set up in London, it did not
limit itself to publishing the Constitutions and simply
regulating the lodges under its control. Mindful of its
obligations, it set up its first charity fund. Such charitable
actions were not restricted to the first Grand Lodge of
England. Its rival the Antients Grand Lodge formed a
Provincial Grand Lodge at Fort St. George in India, which also
promptly established a charity fund. Charity, or relief, is, of
course, one of the three great principles of Freemasonry,
and the various British Grand Lodges have practiced it from
their inception. Individual lodges have their own benevolent
funds to give relief to their members and dependants, and
there are also major centralized charity funds that look after
special groups. The first of these to be founded in England
was established by Chevalier Bartholomew Ruspini, who
was Surgeon Dentist to King George III. He and his Masonic
brethren collected money to found and build a school for the
education of the daughters of indigent or deceased Masons.
A similar charity that clothed and paid for the education of
boys was started in 1798, and this also led eventually to the
building of a boys' school in 1856. In the early nineteenth
century the great Grand Master of the United Grand Lodge
of England, the Duke of Sussex, did not simply restrict
himself to being active within Masonic charities, he also

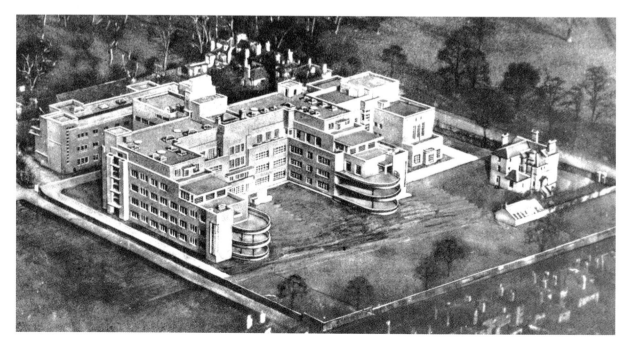

became involved in various Jewish charitable organizations. Later, Queen Victoria became patron of various Masonic charities and donated generously to them on a regular basis. The two educational charities eventually evolved into the Royal Masonic Institution for Girls and the Royal Masonic Institution for Boys. The Royal Masonic Benevolent Institution was created in 1842 to provide annuities or residential care for elderly Freemasons, their widows and dependants. During the First World War, Freemasons founded a hospital in London, and after the war this led to the building of the Royal Masonic Hospital at Ravenscourt Park.

Since the advent of the Welfare State in Britain, the dispensation of charitable monies raised by Masonic bodies has taken a somewhat different course, and various trusts have been established to meet the needs of Masons, their widows, and their children. The dependants' trust provides educational and welfare grants for over one thousand children a year; another trust runs 17 homes for the elderly. The Grand Charity, founded in 1980, has three primary functions: to relieve Masonic petitioners and their dependants; to channel funds to Masonic charities; and to make both major and minor grants to non-Masonic charities.

The Grand Lodge of Ireland created a Central Committee for Charity in 1739, funded by contributions from lodges and public events. The Masonic Female Orphan School was

LEFT: THE ROYAL MASONIC HOSPITAL IN RAVENSCOURT PARK, LONDON, FOUNDED DURING THE FIRST WORLD WAR AND STILL RENDERING STERLING SERVICE IN THE TWENTY-FIRST CENTURY.

ABOVE: QUEEN VICTORIA, WHO BECAME PATRON OF SEVERAL MASONIC CHARITIES AND DONATED GENEROUSLY TO THEM FOR MANY YEARS.

opened in 1802 and a similar school for boys was founded in 1869. Both schools closed down in the 1970s. The proceeds from the sale of these schools now form a trust which provides educational grants for children of both sexes.

Freemasonry has often been accused of restricting its charitable activities so as solely to benefit its own

membership, rather like modern benevolent societies—and in the very beginning that was undoubtedly true. However, from the time of the creation of the first Grand Lodge in England that picture began to change dramatically. In 1731 English lodges raised considerable sums of money to assist poor emigrant families to join General Oglethorpe and settle the colony of Georgia. They also funded the apprenticeship of the orphaned sons of a number of operative Masons. All three of the Grand Lodges in the British Isles contributed

A PIPER IN HIGHLAND DRESS LEADS A PROCESSION OF MEN IN FULL MASONIC REGALIA OUT OF THE STATE OPERA HOUSE OF ST. GEORGE'S, BERMUDA, IN THE CEREMONY OF THE PEPPERCORNS.

funds to assist British prisoners of war in Europe and to help relieve the misery of French prisoners of war in England. In modern times, a trust with a capital sum of over £600,000 was established by the United Grand Lodge of England in 1967 under the administration of the Royal College of Surgeons, to fund medical research into both cancer and heart disease. British Masonic charities have purchased a lifeboat for the Royal National Lifeboat Institution, founded a Chair of Gerontology at Cambridge University, funded

research and welfare projects in the field of drug abuse, and given countless grants to a wide variety of medical charities, as well as subscribing generously to disaster appeals.

In the United States of America, many of the Grand Lodges support homes for elderly Freemasons, their widows, and orphans, as well as providing relief for distressed children of members of the Craft. They have founded charitable institutions that provide scholarships, educational grants for young people in higher education, and vocational grants, irrespective of whether or not the parents of such children have Masonic backgrounds. The track record of Masonic charities in the US when it comes to funding medical research, especially those branches of science investigating diseases of childhood, is truly exceptional. Both the Northern and Southern Supreme Councils of the Scottish Rite have poured vast sums into supporting children's hospitals

that treat all children and not just those with a Masonic father. The Scottish Rite jurisdictions, ably aided by the Shriners, have established specialist burns units and clinics dealing with children affected by language disorders, and all three organizations are rightly renowned for their massive charitable contributions to bodies dealing with handicapped children. American Freemasonry has funded research into children's illness, cancer, schizophrenia, and both alcohol and drug abuse. In 1985, for example, Masonic charities of all jurisdictions contributed over 300 million dollars to support research, medical assistance, and other community projects in which the vast majority of beneficiaries were ordinary citizens with no Masonic affiliation whatsoever.

A similar record of charitable activities could be described for every country where Freemasonry flourishes today. Furthermore, although Freemasonry's charitable record is truly exemplary, charity is but one of its main aims and objectives. Just as the benefits of charitable relief are not restricted solely to Freemasons but instead are extended into the wider communities that Freemasons serve, brotherly love and truth are also dispensed far beyond the boundaries of the Craft, sometimes with an intensely personal effect.

MASONIC MEMBERSHIP

Freemasonry spans the entire free world. Originating in Scotland sometime during the seventeenth century, it crossed into England soon after and created its own formal organization as regular Freemasonry with the foundation of the first Grand Lodge. It has, over the intervening centuries, been praised, extolled, slandered, vilified, imitated, and condemned. This book is directed at ordinary people who know nothing about Freemasonry at all and who are, most probably, still tinged with some degree of bias or suspicion about it. The opinions expressed here are to be analyzed, criticized, and evaluated according to the reader's understanding. Debate is healthy, for little about Freemasonry's origins is written on tablets of stone and much still remains to be discovered. What can be judged fairly in the light of today's knowledge is the Craft and its actions now, in the twenty-first century.

a degree of truth?

THERE IS A COMMON THREAD LINKING ANCIENT EGYPT, BIBLICAL ISRAEL, THE MEDIEVAL KNIGHTS TEMPLAR, AND THE SEVENTEENTH-CENTURY EMERGENCE OF FREEMASONRY IN SCOTLAND, AND THAT LINK IS THE REX DEUS FAMILIES.

Armoiries accordees à L'Ordre des Templiers par le Pape Eugene III.

The origins of Freemasonry are shrouded in the mists of time and can only be vaguely discerned in the teachings of the various hidden streams of spirituality on which it has drawn. Its undoubted debt to the initiatory traditions of Ancient Egypt is recorded in its own rituals, as is its reliance on symbolism, myth, and allegory based upon the Biblical accounts of the building of the Temple of Solomon. Drawing heavily from the Western esoteric tradition, the most profoundly imaginative and influential tradition of European culture, Freemasonry shares insights, teaching, and links with both the philosophy and the mystery cults of ancient Greece. Yet how did it gain something like its present form in the early eighteenth century? What influences linked this relatively modern society with such an ancient past?

REX DEUS

The answer lies with the secretive and influential families of the Rex Deus group who trace their ancestry back to the 24 hereditary families of the *ma'madot*, the hereditary high-priestly families of the temple in Jerusalem. These families which, according to their own accounts, included the family of Jesus, preserved a belief system that was completely at variance with the teachings of the Christian Church. The Church believes that Jesus was God incarnate and came to Earth to redeem us from sin. The Rex Deus belief is that Jesus was a divinely inspired teacher who came to teach us a spiritual pathway that would lead inevitably to a state of spiritual transformation among its followers and enable them to love their neighbors as themselves, irrespective of racial or religious differences. Following this spiritual path would lead to the gift of divinely inspired knowledge, or Gnosis, that at one and the same time would bring a man closer to God and enable him to behave with justice, love, and truth toward his fellow man.

A KNIGHTS TEMPLAR IN HIS WAR
OUTFIT; FEATURED IN PIERRE
DUPUY'S *HISTOIRE DE L'ORDRE
MILITAIRE DES TEMPLIERS*
(BRUSSELS, 1751).

TEMPLAR ORIGINS

DISPUTE HAS RAGED WITHIN FREEMASONRY ABOUT ITS PUTATIVE TEMPLAR ORIGINS. NO DIRECT CONNECTION BETWEEN THE CRAFT AND THE MEDIEVAL ORDER OF THE KNIGHTS TEMPLAR CAN BE ESTABLISHED. THE INDIRECT LINK BETWEEN THE TWO CAN BE FOUND AMONG THE FAMILIES OF REX DEUS, WHO FOUNDED BOTH ORDERS—ALBEIT CENTURIES APART.

THE KNIGHTS TEMPLAR

The foundation of the Knights Templar in the twelfth century was the first visible expression of Rex Deus activity that we can trace in the historical record. Their achievements were truly amazing. Not only did they rise to power and wealth with a speed that can solely be explained as the result of a wide-spread conspiracy, but their military prowess and their business skills were exceptional for their time. Like the initiates of old, the Templars transformed the lives of the communities within which they moved, and, through a combination of their protection of the routes of communication and the creation of their efficient banking system, they laid the true foundations of the capitalist system of modern Europe. Within the Order, true fraternity and absolute obedience were the rules that formed the basis for everything they achieved. Yet while it is tempting for many to propose that Freemasonry arose directly from the heretical Order of the Knights Templar, this is patently absurd, for the military Order was suppressed in 1314 and Freemasonry did not begin to emerge from the shadows until nearly three centuries later. There can be, therefore, no direct link between the medieval Order and modern Freemasonry. Yet Templar thinking and symbolism abounds within the Craft. The question is: how did it get there?

The Rex Deus families once again provide the link. Templar traditions, symbolism, and ritual were preserved among the families who first created the knightly Order, especially in Scotland where the Order survived for some decades after its dissolution elsewhere in Europe. The families of the St. Clairs of Roslin, the Setons, the Stuarts, and the Montgomerys played a major role in keeping

Templar tradition vibrantly alive in Scotland. It was to surface some considerable time later when the appropriate moment and opportunity arose. Thus, while Freemasonry is not the child of the medieval Templar Order, it is a branch from the same genealogical tree; both the Templars and Freemasonry were created by the family group of Rex Deus and, while separated by several centuries, both nonetheless embody the same spiritual principles. Indeed, Earl William St. Clair is the first man that we can positively identify as having the means, the motive, and the opportunity to begin the long, slow process of transformation that changed the late medieval operative guild of stonemasons in Scotland into some embryonic form of Freemasonry. Freemasonry certainly first came to notice in Midlothian, Scotland, sometime in the mid-to-late sixteenth century, and by 1601 had initiated King James VI of Scotland. With him it moved south into England and began to develop into the fraternity that we know today.

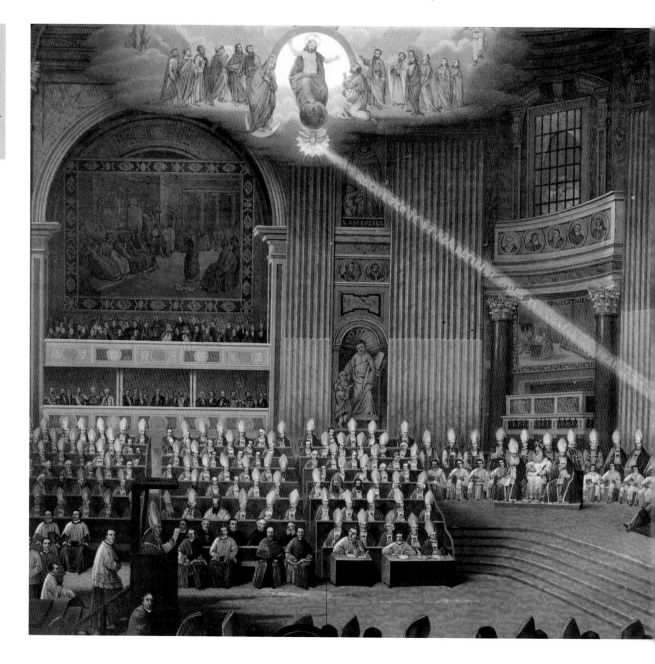

THE ATTITUDE OF THE CHRISTIAN CHURCHES

The Catholic Church has, if nothing else, been consistent in its attitude to the worldwide fraternity of Freemasonry. It condemned it from the very beginning and many Masons suffered at the hands of the Inquisition as a direct consequence of that decision. Pope Pius IX fulminated against the fraternity almost without ceasing, but perhaps he had some personal reasons of his own, having lost all political and temporal power as a result of the unification of Italy. Even today, the Catholic Church still condemns the Craft, and the present Pope, when he headed the Congregation for the Doctrine of the Faith, the modern equivalent of the Inquisition, declared that:

The Church's negative judgement in regard to Masonic associations remains unchanged since their principles have always been considered irreconcilable with the doctrine of the Church and, therefore, membership in them remains forbidden. The faithful who enrol in Masonic associations are in a state of grave sin and may not receive Holy Communion.

If there is anything fundamentally anti-Christian in Freemasonry's teachings and practices, then how is it that so many Anglican priests in England have played such a major role in the Craft over the centuries? While there is some degree of criticism of the fraternity by fundamentalist preachers in many parts of the world, there are also a large

number of ministers and pastors from a wide variety of Protestant groups who enjoy the undoubted spiritual benefits of Masonic membership. Perhaps the root cause of the attitude adopted by the Catholic Church is its insistence that spirituality only exists to gain salvation in this world in order to gain eternal life in the next. Freemasonry, on the other hand, like so many other spiritual paths of proven validity, uses spiritual insight to bring about transformative change in men's lives here on Earth as well as bringing them closer to God, and thereby, perhaps, liberating them from undue dependence on the Church.

FREEMASONRY'S ATTITUDE TO POLITICS

Regular Freemasonry, and its immediate precursors, have always held fast to the double ban on the discussion of either politics or religion in lodge meetings. Indeed, one of the most frequent criticisms of the attitude of the Grand Orient of France is not only that it admits atheists but that it has been lax in enforcing the ban on political discussion and activity by its constituent lodges. However, Freemasons are not merely men, they are also citizens of their various countries and have a duty to take part, as individuals and not as Masons, in the political life of their state. Naturally, they all have their own individual political opinions and many stand for election for public office. They are representative of a complete cross-section of the population and their individual political opinions reflect that fact, and they can and do support the parties of their choice. Freemasonry takes no active part in the political life of any of the countries in which it is established. It does not field candidates, and neither supports nor condemns any political party: it stands resolutely aloof from the entire process.

The political achievements and failures of several individual Masons have been mentioned earlier, and the participation of certain members in the creation of the

Constitution of the United Sates of America and the Declaration of the Rights of Man should not be taken as resulting from political action by the Fraternity. On the other hand, it is perfectly reasonable to view these important documents as expressions of the spiritual values of fraternity imbibed by their various authors from the Masonic tradition.

THE CONSPIRACY THEORISTS

We can trace the beginnings of the various anti-Masonic conspiracy theories directly back to the Abbé Barruel, who claimed that the French Revolution was part of a bloodthirsty plot concocted by Freemasons to overthrow the authority of both Church and State—even though, as we have seen, French Freemasons suffered disproportionately more than the rest of the population because of the preponderance of the wealthy middle classes and aristocrats among its membership. The wild-eyed modern fanatics who propose that Freemasonry allied itself with the Jews to create a New World Order simply ignore reality. If their theory had any truth, the conspiracy they speak of is signally ineffective, for neither Freemason nor Jew has yet been elected Pope, emerged as the leader of any African nation, become head of state in any republic arising from the ashes of the Soviet Union, or become president of an Islamic country anywhere in the world.

THE FRUITS OF INITIATION

The achievements of many individual Freemasons are viewed with pride not merely by Freemasons but by humanity as a whole. The poetry and spiritual insight of Goethe, the musical genius of Mozart, the works of Jean

LATE-NINETEENTH-CENTURY TABLE OF THE BELIEFS AND OBLIGATIONS OF A FREEMASON FROM ONE OF THE FRENCH JURISDICTIONS.

Sibelius, Rudyard Kipling, Jonathan Swift (the author of *Gulliver's Travels*), W. S. Gilbert of Gilbert and Sullivan, Duke Ellington, Winston Spencer Churchill, Robbie Burns, and Irving Berlin are just a small sample of the fruits of Freemasonry made manifest in the creative world.

An important question to ask is, "What are the benefits for the majority of Masons today?" They include companionship, conviviality, a heightened sense of purpose in life, true fraternity on a worldwide scale, and bonding with one's fellows in the lodge in a manner that is truly beyond description. No words can convey the privilege of sharing such an important part of one's life with people of every class, race, creed, and color. The learning that ensues does not simply arise out of the proximity of one's fellows but is imbibed slowly, imperceptibly, and cumulatively at a deep spiritual level from the constant repetition of age-old rituals and teachings imparted with solemnity and grace. Truly, Freemasonry does make good men better. It makes them better people, more responsible citizens, and more devout in their religious practices. Can you envision any other organization that can bring this about with a mixed population of Christians, Jews, Muslims, Hindus, Zoroastrians, and Buddhists?

In a world assailed by fundamentalist terrorism and wars that are perceived as religious in nature, have we not a deep-seated need for true brotherhood, tolerance, justice, and peace? When fundamentalism of either the Christian or Muslim variety preaches hatred, intolerance, violence, and death, do we not need some sanity? Freemasonry has created an unarguably efficient and tried and tested way to inspire men of goodwill to live in peace with one another, and serve their communities with a true generosity of spirit. Masons have learned to ignore the differences that tend to divide mankind and to treasure the common humanity and spirituality that unites us all. That is the true brotherhood that it teaches, founded firmly on the one foundation of truth and justice. Perhaps that is the ultimate result of the search for the Holy Grail.

FURTHER READING

Addison, Charles G., *The History of the Knights Templars*, Adventures Unlimited Press, 1997

Anon., *Secret Societies of the Middle Ages*, Kessinger Publishing, 2003

Armstrong, K., *A History of God*, Ballantine Books, 1994

Ashe, Geoffrey, *The Ancient Wisdom*, Macmillan, 1977

Baigent, Leigh and Lincoln, *The Holy Blood and the Holy Grail*, Dell, 1983

Baigent, Leigh, *The Temple and the Lodge*, Arcade Publishing, 1991

Burman, Edward, *The Inquisition. The Hammer of Heresy*, Sutton Publishing Ltd., 2004

Bussel, F. W., *Religious Thought and Heresy in the Middle Ages*, 2 vols, Kennikat Press, 1971

Campbell, Joseph and Bill Moyers, *The Power of Myth*, Doubleday, 1990

Cannon, Dolores, *Jesus and the Essenes*, Ozark Mountain Publishing, 1999

Christie-Murray, David, *A History of Heresy*, Oxford University Press, 1989

Dafoe, Stephen and Butler, Alan, *The Warriors and the Bankers*, Templar Books, 1998

Desgris, Alain, *L'Ordre des Templiers et la Chevalerie Maçonique Templière*, Guy Trédaniel, 1995

Fortune, Dion, *Esoteric Orders and Their Work*, Weiser Books, 2000

Fox, Robin Lane, *Pagans and Christians*, Knopf, 1987

Gardner, Laurence, *Bloodline of the Holy Grail*, Fair Winds Press, 2002

Godwin, Malcolm, *The Holy Grail*, Bloomsbury, Studio, 1994

Gould's History of Freemasonry, 4 vols, Caxton, 1994

Hamill, John and Gilbert, *World Freemasonry*, HarperCollins, 1992

Jackson, Keith B., *Beyond the Craft*, Lewis Masonic, 2002

Jennings, Hargrave, *The Rosicrucians—Their Rites and Mysteries*, Kessinger Publishing, 1997

Knight, Chris and Lomas, Robert, *The Hiram Key*, Fair Winds Press, 2001

Knight, Chris and Lomas, Robert, *The Second Messiah*, Fair Winds Press, 2001

Knoup, James, *The Genesis of Freemasonry*, Manchester University Press, 1947

Lacroix, P. *Military and Religious Life in the Middle Ages*, University Press of the Pacific, 2003

Lea, H. C., *The Inquisition in the Middle Ages*, 3 vols, Barnes & Noble, 1994

Macintosh, Christopher, *The Rosicrucians*, Crucible, Weiser Books, 1998

Mackenzie, Kenneth, *The Royal Masonic Cyclopedia*, Kessinger Publishing, 2002

Matthews, John, *The Grail Tradition*, Element Books, 1996

Matrasso, Pauline (trans.), *The Quest of the Holy Grail*, Penguin Classics, 1969

HRH Prince Michael of Albany, *The Forgotten Monarchy of Scotland*, Chrysalis Books, 2002

Moore, L. David, *The Christian Conspiracy*, Pendulum Press, 1994

Moore, R. I., *The Formation of a Persecuting Society*, Basil Blackwell, 1990

Murray, David Christie, *The History of Heresy*, Oxford University Press, 1989

Nicholson, Helen, *The Knights Templar*, Sutton Publishing Limited, 2004

Partner, Peter, *The Knights Templar and their Myth*, Destiny Books, 1990

Pauwels, Louis and Bergier, Jacques, *The Dawn Of Magic*, Avon, 1968

Querido, René, *The Mystery of the Holy Grail*, Rudolf Steiner College, 1991

Robinson, John J., *Dungeon, Fire and Sword*, M. Evans and Company, 1992

Robinson, John, *Born in Blood,* M. Evans and Company, 1990

Roszak, Theodore, *Where The Wasteland Ends—Politics and Transcendence in Post-Industrial Society*, Doubleday, 1978

Stevenson, David, *The First Freemasons*, Aberdeen University Press, 1989

Stoyanov, Yuri, *The Hidden Tradition in Europe*, Arkana, 1994

Waite, A. E., *The Holy Kabbalah*, Oracle Publishing, 1996

Wakefield, Walter and Evans, Austin P., *Heresies of the Middle Ages*, Columbia University Press, 1991

Wallace-Murphy, Tim, *An Illustrated Guide Book To Rosslyn Chapel*, The Friends of Rosslyn, 1993

Wallace-Murphy, Tim, *The Templar Legacy and the Masonic Inheritance Within Rosslyn Chapel*, The Friends of Rosslyn, 1994

Wallace-Murphy, Tim and Hopkins, Marilyn, *Rosslyn: Guardian of the Secrets of the Holy Grail*, Element Books, 2003

Wallace-Murphy, Tim, Hopkins, M. and Simmans, G., *Rex Deus*, Editions du Rocher, 2001

Wakefield, L. and Evans, A. P., *Heresies of the Middle Ages*, Columbia University Press, 1969

Ward, J. S. M. *Freemasonry and the Ancient Gods*, Kessinger Publishing, 1996

Wilson, Colin, *The Occult*, Duncan Baird Publishers/Watkins, 2006

GLOSSARY

Acacia An evergreen plant which, within Freemasonry is held to symbolize initiation, immortality, and innocence. Used to mark the burial place of Hiram Abif

Alchemy, alchymical process Philosophical system allegedly intended to create and use metaphysical power for turning base metals into gold as an allegory for the spiritual transformation of the base metal of man to the pure gold of enlightenment

Ancient Craft Masonry The three degrees of Entered Apprentice, Fellow Craft, and Master Mason that are held to be the only degrees practiced by the Craft

Apprentice An indentured learner in a trade or profession—"indentured" by contract to serve out a studentship for a specified time while being taught by a master until proficient enough to be a master himself; a tradition carried on in a nominal way by Craft (Freemason) convention today

Apron The principal clothing of a Freemason adopted from the operative guild of Masons. The first gift bestowed by the Master to the newly Entered Apprentice, made of white lambskin, symbolizing purity

Apsidal end A curved or semicircular extension to a rectangular church that is usually added at the east end of the building and may contain an altar

Ark of the Covenant Originally, the strongbox or chest in which the tablets of stone collected by Moses and containing the Ten Commandments were kept, regarded as most holy and thus stored with due ceremony and security in the Temple of Solomon at Jerusalem; after the destruction of the First Temple, the stone tablets were replaced with scrolls of the Torah

Ashlar Freestone as it comes out of the quarry. Symbolic within Freemasonry in two forms: in its rough, unhewn state, a "rough ashlar", it symbolizes the uncultivated and ignorant condition of mankind; the perfect ashlar, on the other hand, is held to represent the condition of mental health and moral integrity of the spiritual initiate that arises from purifying the mind from all earthly taints. The initiate is "raised" from the figurative death of the mysteries to show spiritual progress

Baphomet Name or title of an idol that the Knights Templar were accused of worshiping in place of God

Benedictine monks Benedictine monks follow the Order of St. Benedict and are mostly—but not essentially—Roman Catholics: the Order is unique in not being formally attached to a specific denomination; within the Order, also following the Rule established by Benedict of Nursia (fl. 530), are the monks and nuns of the Cistercians and the Bernardines

Bethany Village (two miles east of Jerusalem) with personal associations for Jesus the home of Mary, Martha, and Lazarus (all of which may, in an Essene or Nazorean community, represent titles, not names), and thus a possible community center; Luke suggests a further association of the village with the Ascension

Black Madonnas Statues and icon-like paintings of the Virgin Mary as Christ's mother in which her skin color is depicted as dark or black; most date from between the eleventh and fifteenth centuries and are located in churches and shrines particularly associated with miraculous events; theories abound on why the skin color is dark, and include suggestions of earlier traditions relating to mother-goddesses

Catholic Church   The Christian Church, historically based in Rome under the authority of the Pope, but since the sixteenth century fragmented into different denominations many of which now no longer owe allegiance to Rome or even describe themselves as "Catholic" (originally meaning simply "universal")

Chaldeans   Aramaic speakers of ancient southern Mesopotamia who provided several dynasties of the rulers of Babylonia (generally in opposition to the Assyrians)

Cistercian Order   The Cistercian Order was formed in an endeavor both to revert to the original Rule of St. Benedict and to increase the austerity of the required lifestyle with particular reference to manual effort; its most effective leader was Bernard of Clairvaux

Cohens (of ancient Israel)   Priests of the family of Moses' brother Aaron, amounting to a hereditary priestly Order that in many respects (including both duties and prestige) remains current today, especially among Orthodox and Conservative Jews; not to be confused with Levites (although all Cohens are part of that "tribe") or rabbis (who are better described as teachers)

Commonwealth   Term chosen by Oliver Cromwell to describe the form of his and his successors' rule of England in place of a hereditary monarch from 1649 to 1660, intended to denote that it would be for the common good ("well-th")

Copper Scroll of Qumran   Scroll discovered in 1947 listing a certain number of buried or hidden treasures; it was ignored for more than 30 years—partly because of disputes over its orthographic authenticity—until one or two of the "treasures" listed began to turn up; then questions arose over why its orthography was so peculiar, and whether it was because of its Essene origin

Council of Nicea   Council of the Christian Church convened by Constantine the Great in 325 in Nicea (now Iznik, Turkey); one result of it was the Nicene Creed

Crusades   Series of wars undertaken between 1096 and 1291 for religious and political motives by various Christian kings and rulers of European states, sanctioned by contemporary Popes, and nominally intended to free the Holy Land (Palestine) from Muslim overlordship

Dead Sea Scrolls   Assortment of ancient writings unearthed in caves on the western side of the River Jordan mainly between 1947 and 1956, and comprising most of the Old Testament books in much earlier forms than previously discovered, together with a number of other religious texts, apparently hoarded by an Essene community exterminated in CE 68

Declaration of Arbroath   Letter written in Latin dated April 6, 1320 from Scottish nobles to the Pope declaring Scotland to be an independent sovereign nation free to wage war on all invaders (meaning the English, under Edward I and Edward II, who until then had enjoyed the Pope's nominal support); eight years later, possibly under papal pressure, Edward III of England forswore all claims to the throne of Scotland under the Treaty of Northampton

Declaration of the Rights of Man   Fundamental document of the French Revolution setting out the rights of citizens as individuals and collectively; it was formally adopted by the National Constituent Assembly on August 26, 1798; some clauses are very comparable with clauses in the US Constitution promulgated 11 years earlier

Desposyni   Descendants of Jesus Christ through Mary Magdalene; the term is derived from the Greek and literally means "(those) of the Lord"

Druids, Druidic culture   Priests of the ancient Britons, who ritually worshiped in groves of oak trees sacred to the god. Although the word has Celtic cognates, druid derives via Latin from the Greek for "oak tree"

Entered Apprentice   The first degree awarded within Craft or Blue Lodge Freemasonry after a candidate has been properly examined and approved. The foundation of a candidate's progress toward growing moral worth

Erasmus   Dutch-born scholar who was the first to translate the New Testament from Greek, and who around 1500 then became Professor of Divinity and Greek at Cambridge University, England, gaining an international reputation as a humanist and a religious and political commentator

Essenes   Jews who in Jesus' time had their own strict religious rites and ceremonies, and their own established hierarchy and positions in it; the Nazoreans would seem very likely to have been an offshoot of the Essenes

Fellow Craft   This term describes the second degree of Craft or Blue Lodge Freemasonry

French Revolution   Violent civil uprising involving the mass murder of much of the upper and upper-middle classes and the arrogation of their property to "the masses" in urban France, especially Paris, between 1789 and 1799; the monarchy was replaced by a republic, and the Roman Catholic Church in the country was forcibly restructured

Gentiles   Originally, people who were not Jewish and who were therefore "of (another) race" (Latin: *gentilis*)

Gnostic thought   Esoteric compilation of supposedly occult knowledge (gnosis) derived from various early religions and mystery cults, amounting itself to a form of religion that recognized a hierarchy of deities; it was influential on early Christian thought

Golgotha   "Skull(-place)" outside the walls of Jerusalem, where Jesus was crucified; why it was so called is not known, but may have been topographically descriptive; the late Latin name was Calvaria (Calvary), a close translation

Gospel of Thomas   Collection of the sayings of Jesus (including a few "dialogues") often described as a Gnostic document yet quite possibly dating from a time before Gnosticism had genuinely influenced Christian thought; around half of the "sayings" recorded have no known parallel in the canonical New Testament, and some are actually contradictory

Gothic architecture   Style of formal building in Europe between the twelfth and the sixteenth centuries, characterized by interior height featuring pillars, arches, and rib vaulting, and exterior solidity featuring walls supported by flying buttresses; in England, Gothic architecture begins as "Early English," moves through "Decorated," and ends as "Perpendicular"

Great Fire in Rome   Conflagration in July, 64 CE, that raged for a total of nine days and caused massive destruction of property both private and public; it is said that two-thirds of Rome had to be rebuilt; the Emperor Nero was probably absent at the time, but his enjoyment of planning the reconstruction (including his own Domus Aurea) fueled rumors that he had started the blaze himself and extemporized verses accompanying himself on the lyre as he watched

Green Man   An ancient representation of the god of nature which spans nearly all known cultures and that was particularly important to the medieval craftmasons. Believed by many to derive from the ancient Babylonian god Tumuz, who died each Fall and was resurrected in the Spring

Hermetic cults   Cults supposedly based on the writings of followers of Hermes Trismegistos, the Greek name for the Egyptian god Thoth, expounding a mystical philosophy akin to alchemy but influenced also by a dualist system tending toward sun-worship

Holy Grail   Commonly described as the chalice or cup (Old French: *graal*) used at the Last Supper, it has nonetheless also been held instead to symbolize the "holy blood" (medieval French: *sang réal*) of Christ, and therefore of his descendants. Believed by many to be a state of spiritual enlightenment that results from the Gnostic quest

Holy Roman Emperors   Rulers of a widespread but often-changing territory within Europe between 800 and 1806 CE, and crowned as such by the contemporary Pope (so incidentally affirming the Pope's temporal authority); the first thus crowned was Charlemagne, King of the Franks; from 1438 Holy Roman Emperors all belonged to the House of Habsburg, of whom the last ruler was Franz I of Austria

House of David   Dynasty founded by the great Hebrew leader David, who captured Jerusalem and made it his capital in around 1000 BCE

initiation cults/Orders   Gnostic groups who followed a graded path of mysticism with the goal of achieving enlightenment or gnosis and who were intensely secretive

Inquisition   Form of court established by the Catholic Church in 1233 to root out and suppress heretical views; officers of the court held considerable disciplinary powers of investigation and punishment, put to full use notably in Spain between the sixteenth and eighteenth centuries; its current form has since 1965 been formally called the Sacred Congregation for the Doctrine of the Faith

Isis cult   The cult of the Egyptian goddess Isis was originally based on fertility rites that by late Roman times had become immoral; nonetheless, the image of Isis with her son Horus seemed to early Roman Christians to reflect the image of the Virgin Mary with Jesus and may account for some of the Black Madonnas

James the Just, brother of Jesus   A "pillar" of the early Church, first patriarch of Jerusalem, but at all times a promoter of Jewish Christianity rather than the "open" Christianity of Paul; he is called "the Just" because of his strict asceticism (but also to distinguish him from James the Great, ex-fisherman brother of John, and James the Less, brother of Matthew)

John the Baptist   Itinerant preacher and baptizer who announced the coming of one greater than he, and who was in Christian terms thus the final (and according to Jesus, the greatest) prophet of the Old Testament; almost undoubtedly an Essene, his main area of operations was on the banks of the River Jordan close to the caves of Qumran

Joseph of Arimathea   Wealthy citizen of Jerusalem whose private mausoleum was the scene of Jesus' resurrection from the dead; it was he who according to one tradition collected some of Jesus' blood while he was on the Cross in a chalice that then became the Holy Grail, and brought the Grail to England, where he set up the first Christian church at Glastonbury

Kabbala   Also spelled Kabbalah, Cabbala, and Qabbala (among other variants), mystical movement within Judaism intended to elicit and use esoteric knowledge of God and his Creation, with particular reference to finding special meaning in the words of the Tanakh (the Hebrew Bible); some Kabbalist scholars focus entirely on numerological interpretations

Last Supper   Ceremonial meal resembling that of the Passover celebrated by Jesus and his disciples in Jerusalem immediately before the events that were to lead directly to the Crucifixion; during the meal Jesus instituted what became the Christian rite known as the Mass or Holy Communion

Lodge   House at which members of the Freemasonry meet privately, but also the specific organization of the Craft in one state or region, whose headquarters might thus be a Grand Lodge

Magi of Persia   Priestly astronomers and astrologers of Zoroastrianism in ancient times; men who seemed so wise that their knowledge was "magic"

Mandylion   Mystical image of Jesus's face as apparently imprinted upon a cloth, said to have been sent by Jesus to Abgarus of Edessa to heal him of a disability; some 450 years later an image of similar description was discovered in Edessa and was hailed as miraculous, only to be lost during the Persian conquest of the area in 609; by tradition it surfaced once more in the 940s and was taken to Constantinople amid rejoicing; however, it was finally (and somewhat ironically) lost at the sack of that city by the Crusaders in 1204

Mary Magdalene   Mary of Magdala was a follower and devout supporter of Jesus after he had "cast out seven demons" from her; she was also present at the Crucifixion, and was the first witness to the empty tomb on the third day thereafter; so even if she was not Mary of Bethany (sister of Martha and Lazarus, who may or may not also have been the tearful "sinner who repented," later said once to have been a prostitute), she was a fixture in Jesus' circle and may even have been his wife, the mother of his children

Master Mason   The third degree of Craft or Blue Lodge Freemasonry, the most honorable distinction the worldwide Craft can bestow

Mithras   Originally a Vedic folk hero, Mithras became the ancient Persian god of celestial light-in-darkness and associated therefore with life-in-death, or immortality; worship was for men only; in this form, worship of Mithras was introduced to Rome in 68 BCE and he became the war-god of the Roman soldiery (as opposed to Mars, war-god of the Roman senate and state)

Moses Maimonides   Spanish-born twelfth-century Jewish scholar, philosopher and teacher who, influenced by Aristotle, codified Jewish law and ritual practice

Muhammad, the Prophet   Founder of Islam, by revelation the originator of the Koran (Quran; fully compiled after his death in 632), and recognized by adherents as the last and greatest of God's prophets in the sequence listed in the Hebrew Bible but also including Jesus (regarded as no more than his predecessor prophet)

Mystery cults   *See initiation cults/Orders*

Nazoreans   Sect associated with (though not necessarily identified with) the Essenes and thus of Jewish background but with independent religious rites and practices and (probably) even scriptures; it may be that the description of Jesus as a Nazarene or "of Nazareth" was intended to disguise his belonging to the Nazoreans

Numa Pompilius   Second king of ancient Rome, successor to Romulus, reformer of the lunar and solar calendars, founder of the priesthood known as pontifices ("bridge-builders"), and creator of the occupational guilds of the city

Oracle at Delphi   Oracle in ancient Greece originally dedicated to "the Lady" but from early times taken over by the priestesses of Apollo; the oracular speaker sat on a platform above a volcanic vent so that fumes swayed the senses of both priestess and audience; not surprisingly, oracles recorded for posterity tend to make little sense

Orphic cults   Mystery cults based on ancient Greek rites that included "Orphic" hymns that expressed a belief in elements of reincarnation over a sequence of earthly lives so long as an austere lifestyle was maintained

Papal States   Territories within central Italy under the direct, personal rule of the Pope between 756 and 1870 (when Italy became a unified country)

Parliamentarians and Royalists   The two sides in the Civil War in England (and Ireland) between 1642 and 1651, at which time Oliver Cromwell became Lord Protector of the Realm technically on behalf of the Parliamentarians, although the Royalists had two years previously lost their leader and their cause on the execution of Charles I on January 30, 1649

Patriarch of Jerusalem   Originally, the leader of the early Christian community in Jerusalem, but in recent centuries horribly complicated by the number of different national Churches and denominations claiming to be based in the city; the Roman Catholic Archbishop of Jerusalem is thus (since 1847) entitled to be called the Patriarch, although in the eyes of most Christians the Patriarch of Jerusalem is in fact the leader there of the Eastern Orthodox Church; a third such is the Armenian Patriarch of Jerusalem, leader of the Armenian Apostolic Church

Paul (Saul of Tarsus)   Self-appointed Christian apostle whose ideas and methods transformed the Jewish-oriented beliefs and rites of early Christianity into the "open" Church it has been now for millennia; Paul himself was a well-educated Roman citizen with friends (and probably relations) in high places; it was he and his Greek-speaking associates who ensured the documentation of his version of Christianity

Peter (Simon Peter; Cephas)   Jesus' disciple, the "big fisherman" who became spokesman for them all after Jesus' Ascension, and who thereafter traveled widely with the Gospel message, probably to Rome where, by tradition, he is regarded as the first bishop; as described, he is among the most human characters of the New Testament scriptures, not at all like the "rock" after which he was nicknamed by Jesus ("Peter," "Cephas")

Pharisees   Devout (but not fundamentalist) adherents of Jewish traditions from a couple of centuries before Jesus; they were particularly opposed to Greek culture and, by association therewith, to Roman rule, although in general they were not in favor of political action; unlike the more fundamentalist Sadducees, the Pharisees looked forward to the coming of a Messiah and believed in the eventual resurrection of the dead

Puritans   Members of the Church of England in the sixteenth and early seventeenth centuries who wished their Church to eliminate all elements of "Catholic" practices, including supervision by bishops; a high proportion wanted to change the Church rather than leave it altogether

Reformation   Fundamental change in historical and philosophical view of a major part of the Western Christian Church during the sixteenth century, by which it rejected much of what it regarded as unnecessary "accretions" of belief and ritual then current in the Catholic Church; because the leaders of the movement were effectively protesting against submitting to the dogmatic authority of the Pope, their followers became known as Protestants

Renaissance   "Rebirth" of scientific learning in Europe that spread primarily from Italy in around 1400 and radiated outward for the next 200 years or so, notable especially in works of art and literature but also in a new sense of scientific curiosity

Rex Deus   Name (meaning "king god") for the European branch of the bloodline purportedly traceable back to the descendants of

Jesus and Mary Magdalene, and thence back to King David and thence even further back to Moses' brother Aaron

Roman Empire   Roman "national state" and occupied territories from the time of the first formal imperator (Emperor) Augustus Caesar in 27 BCE to the fifth century CE

Romanesque architecture   Also called Norman architecture, a style of building that featured rounded arches, massive piers and barrel-roofing

Roman Republic   Roman "national state" and occupied territories from the traditional date 510 BCE (the expulsion of Tarquinius Superbus, the Etruscan king) to the formal founding of the Roman Empire by Augustus (formerly Octavian) Caesar in 27 BCE

Rosicrucians   Followers of a group of seventeenth-century philosophers who made use of alchemical terms and ideas to claim occult powers; the leading writer of the group called himself Christian Rosenkreutz—hence the name Rosicrucians

sacred geometry   The imputing of religious meaning to mathematical relationships, in particular with reference to the positioning and proportions of human figures in works of art

St. Clair family   Norman French family granted land around Rosslyn, Scotland, by Malcolm Canmore in 1068 when William de St. Clair accompanied the Saxon princess Margaret north to her marriage with the Scottish king; later St. Clairs became the Earls of Orkney, the first of whom may or may not have led an expedition to North America in 1389 (a century before Columbus)

Septimania   Kingdom created by Theodoric the Visigoth in 509 CE, territorially corresponding roughly to the current French region of Languedoc-Roussillon; Theodoric's son married a Merovingian princess, through whose family the kingdom was finally lost to the (Catholic) Franks; at the beginning of the twenty-first century there was a concerted effort by some local politicians to revive the name for the area (in French, Septimanie)

Solomon's Temple in Jerusalem   First Temple built by the ancient Hebrews after capturing and occupying Jerusalem, which then became the Israelites' capital; the inspiration of King David, it was built around 966 BCE under the direction of his son Solomon primarily to house the Ark of the Covenant, symbolizing the "contract" between God and His Chosen People; it was razed to the ground in 587 BCE at the time of the Babylonian Exile

Stuart monarchs   The Stuart royal family inherited the Scottish throne in 1371 (Robert [the] Bruce) and the English throne in 1603 (James VI of Scotland was James I of England); Queen Anne's death in 1714 saw the end of the family's sovereignty and the accession of the House of Hanover

Sufis and Sufism   Mystical movement within Islam comprising several "denominations" that have their own rites and practices, most of which focus on intuitive meditation; the lifestyle is austerely ascetic, intended to reflect a disdain for material property

Telluric power   Energy radiating from a network or grid beneath the surface of the Earth and concentrated at points where the lines of the network intersect; certainly there are telluric electrical currents (just as there is atmospheric electricity above the Earth's surface), but many believe that ley lines also emit telluric power

Thoth   Ancient Egyptian ibis-headed god, wise scribe, and judge of the Underworld, associated therefore with the secret of life and death

Torah   First five books of the Hebrew Bible, corresponding to Genesis, Exodus, Leviticus, Numbers, and Deuteronomy (the Pentateuch) in the Old Testament; scrolls containing the Torah are reverently housed in an "ark" (a tabernacle) in every synagogue

Zeus   Supreme deity of the Hellenic Greeks, god of daylight and the airy sky and whose home was therefore on top of the highest massif in Greece, Mt. Olympus. This was often shrouded in thick cloud, so Zeus was associated with thunder and lightning too)

Zoroaster   Ancient Persian teacher and reformer who in the early sixth century BCE formulated a dualist religion centered on Ahura Mazda (Ormuzd) and Angra Mainyu (Ahriman), divine forces for good and for evil respectively, involving also a reverence for fire and an expectation of a Last Day on which the dead rise

INDEX

A

Abaris the Druid 11
Abif, Hiram 54, 64–66, 114
Adams, John...........................62, 92
Adoniram.. 64
African Lodge................................. 117
agnus dei.. *53*
Agrippa, Heinrich Cornelius............... 69
Alamo, siege.................................... 99
Albano, Cardinal Matthew d' 28
alchemy.............................38, 62, 132
Allegro, John 27
Alsace, Philippe d' 41
America 62, 108–109, 117
    charity 121
    Constitution 62, 90–93
    Declaration of Independence........ 90
    War of Independence..............86–90
Amiens Cathedral...................34, 38–39

Ancient Accepted Free Masons of
    Scotland....................................72, 81
Ancient and Accepted Rite..........81, 96
Ancient Greece 8–15, 123
Anderson, Dr. James ....
    ....71, 72, 87, 107, 113
Anderson, William.......................36, 58
Andrea, Johann Valentin................... 61
Anjou, Count Fulk d' 64
Annuity Fund 118
Antients Grand Lodge............................
    .... 74–75, 80, 81, 85, 100–101, 118
apprentice 33, 114, 132
Apprentice Pillar 54–55, 56
aprons........................... 102, 103, 114
apsidal end...................................... 132
Ark of the Covenant............. 26–27, 132
army traveling warrants..............74, 85
Arthurian legend 43
Ashmole, Elias 68, 69, 70
Athelstan, King 33, 72

B

Baigent, Michael 43, 82–83
Bakunin.. 98
Baldwin I, King..............................26, 27
Baldwin II, King 25, 27, 28, 64
banks, Templar 30–31
Baphomet 53, 132
Barruel, Abbé............................94, 127
Batham, Cyril N. 81

Batt, Sergeant John 117
Baudouin of Brittany *see* Baldwin I,
    King Beauséante 53, 59
Begg, Ean 44
Benedictine monks.................33, 132
Bérage, Chevalier de 81–82
Best, Peter.. 117
Bethany 132
Bishop of Rome *see* Popes
Bisol, Geoffroi 25
Black Madonnas 37, 38, 44, 46, 54,
    132
Boston Tea Party 88, 89, 90
Botticelli.. 61
Bouillion, Geoffroi de........................ 23
Bouillion, Godfroi de 26, 27, 81
Bruno, S. T. 30
burial practices 38

C

Caggar, Georges 44
Cali, François 38
Calvi, Roberto.................................... 85
Campbell, Professor Joseph 42, 43
Canton, John.................................... 117
Carbonari 97
Catholic Church ..7, 19, 51, 69, 125, 132
    Chevalier Ramsay.......................... 81
    French Revolution 94
cayennes 33
Chaldeans.................................. 11, 132

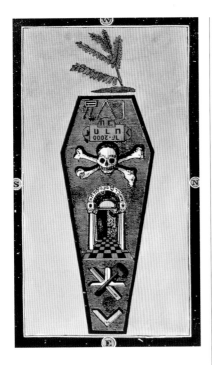

Clifford, Lord 82
Cohens 23, 132–133
Colfs, J. F. 34
Commonwealth 69, 71, 133
Compagnonnage 23, 33, 62
Compagnonnage Tuscana 34
companion 33
Compostela, Archbishop of 48
Constantine the Great, Emperor .. 18–19
Coomeraswamy, Ananda 43
Copper Scroll 27, 133
Correspondence Societies 93
Counts of Champagne 24–25
    see also Hughes, Count of
    Champagne
Cox, David 86
Craftmasons   23, 31–39, 51, 54–55,
    57, 67
Critchlow, Keith 36
croix celeste *53*
croix pattée *26, 53*
Cromwell, Oliver 69, 71
Cross of Lorraine 26
Crucifixion 16, 37
Crusades ....
    23, 25, 29, 36, 42–43, 77–78, 82, 133
crypt, Rosslyn Chapel 57–58

D

Dance of Death 57
Danton, Georges 93
Darius, King 54
David, King of Scotland 28
Dead Sea Scrolls 27, 63, 133
Declaration of Arbroath 81, 88, 91, 133
Declaration of the Rights of Man ....
    ....93–94, 133
Deraismes, Maria 104
Derwentwater, Earl of 82
Desmoulins, Camille 93
Desposyni 17, 133

charity 61, 118–121
Charlemagne 21
Charles I, King 61, 69
Charles II, King 71
Charlie, Bonnie Prince 76, 77, 82, 89
Charney, Geoffroi de 48
Chartres Cathedral 26–27, 34, 35, 37,
    41, 58
Children of Father Soubise 33
Children of Master Jacques 33
Children of Solomon 23, 33–34, 36, 54
Chrétien de Troyes 41, 42
Christianity
    see also Catholic Church
    birth of 16–21
    Holy Grail 43
    ignorance 14, 21, 70–71
    Rex Deus 23
Cistercians 23, 25, 29, 34, 132
civil war 69
Clairvaux, St. Bernard of 23, 24,
    25, 26, 28, 29, 34, 44
Clement V, Pope 47, 49

Druids 16, 133
Dunlop, Ian 33

E

Ebionites 17, 20
Edouard, Abbot 25
Edward VII, King 125
Edwin, Prince 72
Egypt 10, 15, 123
el Khidir 33, 58
Entered Apprentice (First Degree) ....
    .... 113, 114
Erasmus 69, 133
esoteric movement 7, 53, 61, 62,
    69, 123
Essenbach, Wolfram von 42, 44
Essenes 10, 16, 17, 67, 133

F

Fellow Craft Mason
    (Second Degree) 113, 114
First Degree *see* Entered Apprentice
Fisher King 42
Fludd, Robert 61
Fontaine, Bernard de *see* Clairvaux, St.
    Bernard of
Ford, Gerald R. 90
Fort Newton, Joseph 113
France 46–49, 62, 96–97, 104
    Chevalier Ramsay 76–81
    Revolution 93–95, 127, 133
Franklin, Benjamin 62, 85, 86–87
Freeman, Peter 117
Fulcanelli 34, 37

G

Galileo 70
Gardner, Laurence 81
Garibaldi, ... 97, 98
Gedricke 56
gentiles 17, 133

George I, King 71

George, St. ... .58, 59

Georgia 120

Gettings, Fred 34

Gnosis 10, 38, 58, 59, 61, 122

Gnostic thought 8, 9, 10–12, 20, 37, 133

Goethe, Johann 98

Golden Book 37

Golgotha 133–134

Gondemar 25

Gospel of Thomas 38, 43, 134

Gothic architecture 34–37, 134

Grand Charity 119

Grand Lodge of British Columbia 113

Grand Lodge Charity Fund 118

Grand Lodge of England 74, 83, 86, 107

see also United Grand Lodge of England charity 118, 120

Grand Lodge of France 96–97

Grand Lodge of Ireland 72, 74, 85, 102, 119–120

Grand Lodge of Massachusetts 109–110

Grand Lodges 72, 107
role 113

Grand Master 28, 64, 71, 73, 107

Grand Orient of France 96–97, 104, 126

Grant, H. B. 109

Grattan, Henry 98

Graves, Robert 33, 72

Great Fire in Rome 18, 134

Green Man 58, 59, 134

H

Hall, Prince 117

Hancock, John 88, 89

hekaloth 16

Heredom, Lodge of 81–82

heresy 19, 21, 22–23, 42, 43–44, 47

Hermes Trismegistos 10, 53

Hermetic cults 9, 10, 61, 134

Herodian Temple 63, 64

Hiramic legend of the Third Degree 110

Holy Grail 40–49, 134

Holy Roman Emperors 134

Honorius II, Pope 28

"hopscotch" symbol 59

House of David 17, 64, 134

Howard, Foten 117

Hughes, Count of Champagne .. 23, 24–25, 26, 27, 64

I

Ibn Arabi 33

India 117

Indissolubisten 69

initiation 106, 114
alchemy 38
Chartres Cathedral 37
Christians 16
Holy Grail 42
la langue verte 34
rites 11
Rosslyn Chapel 53, 59
Sufis 33

initiation (mystery) cults 8, 9, 10, 14–15, 134

Innocent II, Pope 28

Inquisition 47, 125, 134

International compact 102

Invisible College 51, 69, 93

the Invisibles 69

Iraneus 17

Irish Grand Lodge 72, 74, 85, 102, 119–120

Ishtar 58, 59

Isis cult 10, 15, 134

Italy, reunification 97–99

J

Jackson, General Andrew 87

Jacobites 71, 77, 81, 82, 83

Jacquin 33

James II, King 77

James the Just 16, 17, 20, 64, 134

James VI, King of Scotland (James I of England) 60, 61, 72, 124

Jefferson, Thomas 62

Jerusalem 29
fall of 17
Herodian Temple 63, 64
Temple destruction 64

La Jérusalem Dcossaisse 104

Jesus 16–17, 18, 19, 37, 38, 44, 123
Holy Grail 41, 42, 43

jewels 102, 111

Jews 16, 17, 46, 102, 127

John the Baptist 38, 39, 102, 134

John the Evangelist 102

Johnson, Cyrus 117

Johnson, Paul 17

Jones, John Paul 87

Jordan, Guy 38

Joseph of Arimathea 41, 135
Journeyman's Pillar 56

K

Kabbala 33, 135
Kent, Duke of 101
Kerensky, ... 98
Kilmarnock, Earl of 82
Kilwinning 61, 66, 79, 82
The King of Terrors 57
Knight, Chris 64
Knight of the East degree 64
Knight of the East and
    West degree 64
Knight of the Red Feather 82–83
Knight of the Sword degree 64
Knight White Eagle 63
Knights Hospitallers 49
Knights of St. John 81, 82
Knights Templar 7, 23, 25–31, 33–34,
        36, 64, 81–82, 123–124
        Amiens 38
        Black Madonnas 44
        Friday 13th 46–49
        Holy Grail 40–49
        Pope Pius IX 98
        Scotland 49–59
        suppression 67
Kyot of Provence 44

L

Lafayette, Marquis de 88, 93–94
landmarks 107–113
la langue verte 34
Last Supper 135
Leigh, Richard 43, 83
Leo III, Pope 21
Leo XIII, Pope 97
Leonardo da Vinci 61
Lion's Paw grip 115
Locke, John 91

Lodge of Reconciliation 101
Loge Libres Penseurs 104
Lomas, Robert 64
Longinus, St. 58, 59

M

Mackey, Albert 107–108
Magi of Persia 10, 11, 135
Mallory, Thomas 43
ma'madot 17, 20, 59, 123
Mandylion 58, 135
Marie, Countess of Champagne 41
Martin, Dr. George 104
Mary Magdalene 44, 135
Mary, Queen 69
Masonic Orphan Schools 119–120
Master Mason (Third Degree)...33, 107,
        110, 111–112, 113, 114–115
Master Mason's Pillar 55, 56
Mauritius, St. 58, 59
May Queen 59
Mazzini, ... 97, 98
Melchizedek 41
merkabah 16
Michael the Archangel, St. 58
Mithraic cult 15, 18
Mithras 135
Mitrinovic, Dimitrije 63
Molay, Jacques de 47, 48–49
Montague, Duke of 72
Montbard, André de 23, 25, 26
Montdidier, Payen de 25, 26, 41
Montesquieu, ... 91, 92
Montgomery, Alexander 83
Moody, William 117
Moray, Sir Robert 70
Moses Maimonides 135
Most Equitable Most Sovereign
        Prince Master 64
Muhammad, the Prophet 135
mukhammas 36

Munz, P. 21
mystery cults see initiation cults
mythology 43

N

Nablus, Council of 26
Napoleon Bonaparte 97
Nazoreans 135
Nero, Emperor 16, 18
Nicea, council of 19, 133
Notre Dame cathedral 44
Notre Dame de la Belle Verrière 37
Numa Pompilius 34, 135

O

O'Connell, Daniel 98
odium theologicum 18, 67
Oglethorpe, General 120
Oliver, George 108
oracle at Delphi 21, 135
orden der Unzertrennlichen 69
Orphan Annuity Fund 118
Orpheus 10
Orphic cults 10, 136
Ouspensky, ... 36–37

P

P2 affair 85
Paine, Thomas 91
papal states 136
Parliamentarians 69, 136
passing ceremony 114
Past Master degree 63
Patriarch of Jerusalem...23, 26, 64, 136
Paul, St. 16–18, 136
Pauline Christianity 16–19
Payen, Hughes de 23, 25–26, 27–28,
        29, 41
Payne, George 107
Perceval 41
Perfect Master degree 64

Peter (disciple)................................. 136

Pharisees... 136

Philippe le Bel, King..............46–47, 49

pilgrims, protection.....................26, 30

Pius IX, Pope 97–98, 125

Plato... 11

Popes.............................. 14, 20–21, 97

   see also individual popes

Posidonius.. 11

Pound, Roscoe.................................. 110

Preston, William 107

Price, Henry.. 86

Priscillian of Avila 19

prisoners of war 120

Proctor, Edward 88, 89

Protestants.........................69, 125–126

Provincial Grand Masters............ 72, 86

Puritans... 136

Pythagoras... 11

R

Rachi 24

racial prejudice 116–117

Radclyffe, Charles............................... 82

Raine, Kathleen 43

Ramsay, Chevalier.......................76–81

Randford, Teresa................................. 52

Ravenscroft, Trevor 42, 44

Rayden, Prince................................... 117

Rayner Johnson, Kenneth.................. 34

Rees, Prince 117

Reformation 136

Renaissance 61, 136

retro-choir 56, 57

Revere, Paul 87, 88, 89

Rex Deus 24–25, 27, 28, 48, 66–67,
   122–123

   Charlemagne 21

   Counts of Champagne 24–25

   definition..................................... 136

   European influence 28

Holy Grail.......................... 41, 42, 44

   marital alliances 23

   Masonic ritual 62–64

   origin... 20

   Renaissance 61

Rosslyn Chapel 59

   Scotland.. 51

Rheims Cathedral............................... 34

Righteous Seed............................63–64

Rite of Strict Observance......62, 82, 83

rituals 123

   Masonic 62–64

   purging 64

Robert the Bruce, King 56, 57

Robin, Jean 44

Robinson, John.................................... 67

Roman Empire 12–13, 14–15, 16, 136

Roman Republic................................. 136

Romanesque architecture.........36, 136

Rosicrucians 51, 53, 61, 62, 69, 137

Rossal.. 25

Rosslyn Chapel....41, 50, 51, 52–59, 61,
   64, 66

Roszak, Professor Theodore................ 7

Royal Arch degrees............61, 101, 102

Royal House of Flanders..............23, 26

Royal Masonic Benevolent
   Institution................................... 119

Royal Masonic Hospital 118, 119

Royal Masonic Institution for
   Girls/Boys 119

Royal Society 51, 69, 70, 71

Royalists 136

Roznak, Theodore.............................. 51

Ruform, Duff 117

Ruspini, Chevalier Bartholomew.... 118

Russell, Bertrand 9, 14

S

sacred geometry....................................
   .... 27, 33, 34, 35–36, 137

St. Amand, Achambaud de 25, 26

St. Clair of Roslin, Henri de............... 23

St. Clair of Roslin, Earl Henry............ 54

St. Clair of Roslin, Earl William.............
   ......51–52, 54, 59, 61, 66, 72–74, 124

St. Clairs of Roslin..................................
   .... 23, 28, 51–59, 72, 137

index

St. Leger, Elizabeth.........................104
St. Omer, Geoffroi de..................25, 26
St. Omer, Hughes de.........................26
Santerson, Thomas..........................117
Savoy, House of.................................48
science..70
Scotland.28, 49–59, 61–62, 63, 81, 124
    charity..118
    Grand Lodge 72, 86, 102
    rebellion 71, 82
    Templars trial...........................47–48
Scott, Captain James 117
Scottish Rite Freemasonry ...61, 81, 83,
    121
Seborga 25
Second Degree see Fellow Craft Mason
Secret Master degree 63
Septimania 137
Setons 23
Sieyés, Abbé 93
signatures.....................................33, 34
Sinclairs cross....................................53
Sinncler, William de 53
Slinger, Bueston...............................117
Smith, Boston 117
Socrates 11, 14
Sol Invictus.................................15, 18
solar worship 15
Solomon, King 23, 34, 64
Solomon's Temple..............................
    ....25, 33, 54, 64, 82, 137
Son of the Widow 55–56, 59
Sons of Dawn...............................63–64
Sons of Liberty...........................88, 89
sophia 38
Speain, Cato 117
stained-glass windows,
    Rosslyn Chapel 58–59
Stamp Act...88
Stapelbrugge, Stephen de..................47
Stella Templum...................................83

Stephen, King.....................................28
Strachan, Gordon...............................36
Sufis/Sufism..
    ....30, 31, 33, 36, 44, 58, 137
Supreme Council of the Ancient and
    Accepted Scottish Rite....................96
Sussex, Duke of 101, 102, 118–119
symbolism...
    ....67, 110, 111–112, 115, 123
    Amiens 38
    Rosslyn Chapel 53–54, 56, 59, 66

T
Talleyrand...98
Tammuz.......................................58, 59
telluric power..............................37, 137
Temple Mount..................25, 26–27, 36
Theodosius, Emperor 19
Third Degree see Master Mason
Third Force 69
Thompson, Charles.............................62
Thoth..10, 137
les Tignarii 34
Tiler, Benjamin.................................117
time immemorial lodges 85
Titley, Richard..................................117
Torah 17, 137
Tour de France 33
trade routes 30, 31
Trigance 38
Troyes, Council of.........................28, 44
Tschoudy, Baron 82
Tyre, Guillaume de 25

U
United Grand Lodge of England............
    ....7, 63, 74, 81, 82, 100–105, 113
    charity...121
    France 97

V
Veil of Veronica see Mandylion
Veronica, St. 58
Verrochio 61
Victoria, Queen 119
Villiers, Gerard de 47
Virgin of the Pillar.............................37
Virgini Pariturae................................37
Visconti dukes....................................97
Voltaire 87, 91
von Hund, Baron Karl Gotthelf..........82
Vulgate Cycle.....................................43

W
Warren, Joseph 88, 89
Warren, Lieutenant.............................26
Washington, George 62, 88, 89, 90
Wilins, Dr. John 70
Wilson, Colin 9
women 104–105
Worshipful Master 114–115

Z
Zadok 63–64, 67
Zerubabel, Prince................................54
Zerubabel's Temple............................64
Zeus...9, 137
Zoroaster...................................10, 137

ACKNOWLEDGMENTS

PICTURE CREDITS

The publishers would like to thank the following agencies and institutions for permission to use their images. Every effort has been made to trace the copyright holder, but if there are any omissions, then please contact the publisher.

Art Archive/Musée du Grand Orient/Marc Charmet: 98 right, 111

Bridgeman Art Library: 24; Bibliotheque Nationale, Paris, France: 6, 126; British Library: 48; Forbes Magazine Collection, New York, USA: 119; Hall of Representatives, Washington D.C, USA: 91; Musee du Grand Orient de France, Paris, France, Archives Charmet: 106; National Gallery, UK: 70; O'Shea Gallery, London, UK: 13; Prado, Madrid, Spain, Giraudon: 47 bottom; Private Collection: 62, 88, 104; Roy Miles Fine Paintings: 60; Scottish National Portrait Gallery, Edinburgh, UK: 76

Corbis/Adam Wolfitt: 35; Araldo de Luca: 18, 19; Archivo Iconografico, SA: 21; Bettman: 9, 29; Bradley Smith: 116; Bruce Adams/Eye Ubiquitous: 120; Jon Hicks: 12; Origlia Franco/Corbis Sygma: 45; Ruggero Vanni: 30; Sandro Vannini: 10 top; Tibor Bognar: 14

Getty Images: 49, 50

Grand Lodge of British Columbia: 1, 3, 5, 10 bottom, 51 top right, 59 left, 61, 67, 69, 72 bottom, 90, 97, 102 bottom, 117, 121, 127

Reproduced by kind permission of the Grand Lodge of Scotland: 51 bottom left, 100

John Rushton: 33

Copyright, and reproduced with the permission of the Library and Museum of Freemasonry: 65, 66, 68, 72 top, 74, 78, 80, 84, 86 top, 109, 111, 115, 118, 125, 129

Musee de Nationaux de France: 42

Niven Sinclair: 96

Rosslyn Templars: 55

Tim Wallace-Murphy: 11, 25, 36, 38 bottom, top, 39, 40, 52, 53, 54, 56, 57, 58, 59 right

TopFoto: 63, 83, 92, 101, 108, 128; Charles Walker: 15, 16, 17, 22, 27, 46, 89, 103, 112; Dave Walsh: 102 top; Fortean: 122; Fotomass: 31; HIP/The British Library: 43, 71, 86 bottom; John Baker: 32; Roger Viollet: 94, 98 left, 124

AUTHOR ACKNOWLEDGMENTS

No author can write a book of this nature without assistance and I would like to express my gratitude to all of the people whose ideas, insight, and information have made this volume possible. I would like to pay tribute to three wonderful men who are now sadly no longer with us: Trevor Ravenscroft, Michael Bentine, and James Whittal. I would also like to thank Stuart Beattie of the Rosslyn Chapel Trust; Nicole Dawe of Okehampton, Devon; Richard Beaumont of Staverton, Devon; Dr. Angelo Beneveinto of Vaerse; Robert Brydon of Edinburgh; Jean-Michel Garnier of Chartres; Robert Loman of Bradford; James Mackay Munro of Penicuick; Andrew Pattison of Edinburgh; and Niven Sinclair of London. I also wish to acknowledge the kind assistance of my publisher, David Alexander, editor Rebecca Saraceno, and designer Nicola Liddiard.